Know It, Show It

GRADE 5

Printed in the U.S.A.

ISBN 978-0-358-19210-7

11 12 13 14   0909   26 25 24 23

4500865823   DEFG

r7.20

Grade
5

Contents

Name _____

Short Vowels

▶ **Read each sentence. Find the words that include short vowel sounds. Underline the letters in each word that make a short vowel sound.**

1. We went to Sunset Park to play soccer.

2. John dreaded the chore of dusting the lampshades.

3. Let's go see that film about giraffes and chimpanzees.

4. Henry just wants to play video games.

5. I read about a student who raised funds for class projects.

6. Should I spread butter on your sandwich?

7. Sit silently until the buzzing noise stops.

8. When you finish, please raise your hand.

Name _____

Critical Vocabulary

You can use the words you learn from reading as you talk and write.

> Use details from *The Inventor's Secret* to support your answers to the questions below. Then use the Critical Vocabulary words as you talk with a partner about your answers.

1. What can something that is **incandescent** help you to do?

   _____

2. Name something that is shaped like a **cylinder**.

   _____

3. What does Thomas do to learn more about **locomotives**?

   _____

4. What devices that we use today are similar to the **phonograph**?

   _____

5. Describe what happened when Henry's engine **sputtered**.

   _____

6. Which of Henry's inventions was a **flop**?

   _____

7. Why might inventors want to get **patents**?

   _____

8. What **gadgets** did Thomas invent?

   _____

9. Would you be more likely to say that an airplane or a train **chugged** along? Why?

   _____

> Choose two of the Critical Vocabulary words and use them in a sentence.

   _____

Name _____

Author's Purpose

The **author's purpose** is the author's reason for writing a story or text. Authors usually write to persuade, to inform, to entertain, or to teach a lesson. Knowing a writer's purpose helps readers recognize the author's message.

> ▶ Answer the question about page 19 of *The Inventor's Secret*.

1. What words and actions in this part of the story show that the author wants to entertain readers?

   _____

   _____

> ▶ Answer the question about page 20 of *The Inventor's Secret*.

2. What words and actions in the text show that the author wants to entertain readers?

   _____

   _____

> ▶ Answer these questions about page 30 of *The Inventor's Secret*.

3. What is the author's purpose in the writer's note that follows the story?

   _____

   _____

4. How do you know?

   _____

   _____

Name _____

Short Vowels

> Read each sentence. Under the blank is a reference to a short vowel sound. Find that category of words in the box, and read the two words in that category. Choose the word that completes the sentence best and write it in the blank.

short *a* words	maximum, fracture
short *e* words	spectator, sensation
short *i* words	invisible, twinkling
short *o* words	tropical, prosperous
short *u* words	subsequent, bustling

1. The _____ city was filled with people, cars, and noise.
   short *u* sound

2. Viruses are _____ without the help of a microscope.
   short *i* sound

3. The stars appear to be _____ in the night sky.
   short *i* sound

4. Last week Mike was a _____ at his friend's baseball game.
   short *e* sound

5. The successful business was _____ .
   short *o* sound

6. The Ruiz family enjoyed their _____ vacation.
   short *o* sound

7. The team lost their first game but won all their _____ games.
   short *u* sound

8. Keshia remembered the _____ of cold water on her skin.
   short *e* sound

9. A _____ of 100 people will fit in the room.
   short *a* sound

10. The fall caused a _____ in the athlete's arm.
    short *a* sound

Name _____

Prefixes ex- / e-, Greek Root phon

The word *phonograph* contains a root that has Greek origins. The meaning of the root *phon* is "sound." The prefixes *ex-* and *e-* (meaning "out of, from, or away") are found in words such as *exploded*, *experiment*, and *elongate*.

▶ Complete the chart with other words that contain either the root *phon* or the prefixes *ex-* and *e-*.

phon
_____
_____
_____
_____
ex- / e-
_____
_____
_____

▶ Choose one word from each category and use it in a sentence.

_____

_____

_____

_____

_____

_____

Name _____

Point of View

Point of view describes who is telling a story, either a character in the story (first person) or an outside narrator (third person). A narrator who knows everything is called an omniscient narrator and uses pronouns like *he*, *she*, and *they*. A narrator who is a character in the story uses pronouns like *I*, *me*, *we*, *us*, and *our*.

> **Answer these questions about page 18 of *The Inventor's Secret*.**

1. Who is telling the story—Thomas and Henry or a narrator?

_____

2. How do you know?

_____

_____

> **Answer these questions about page 30 of *The Inventor's Secret*.**

3. What is the point of view of the author's note at the end of the story?

_____

4. How do you know?

_____

Name _____

Central Idea

Central idea is the most important thought of a story or text that is supported by relevant details. Sometimes an author clearly states the central idea. Sometimes it's implied, or suggested, and the reader has to figure it out using evidence in the text.

> **Answer the questions about page 29 of *The Inventor's Secret*.**

1. What is the central idea of the selection?

_____

_____

2. What relevant details in the text support the central idea?

_____

_____

3. How did the author organize the text to support the central idea?

_____

_____

_____

Name _____

Long a and e

> Read each sentence. Find the word that includes the long *a* or the long *e* vowel sound. Underline the vowel or vowel team that makes the sound. Below the sentence, underline "long a sound" or "long e sound."

1. Luis and Ling went to the park to play on the swings.

       long *a* sound   long *e* sound

2. The dog is afraid of cats and kittens.

       long *a* sound   long *e* sound

3. Will you meet us in the backyard after practice?

       long *a* sound   long *e* sound

4. The prefix in the word *express* is *ex–*.

       long *a* sound   long *e* sound

5. Nicole wants to travel to outer space.

       long *a* sound   long *e* sound

6. Jin was born in April, but her sister was born in October.

       long *a* sound   long *e* sound

7. I think it will be easy to finish this assignment.

       long *a* sound   long *e* sound

8. I heard the little boy shriek when a spider crawled on his arm.

       long *a* sound   long *e* sound

9. Tim likes to dip his apple in honey.

       long *a* sound   long *e* sound

10. Ask the clerk for a receipt.

       long *a* sound   long *e* sound

Name _____

Critical Vocabulary

You can use the words you learn from reading as you talk and write.

> Use what you know about the vocabulary words from *Winds of Hope* to help you finish each sentence.

1. You might be **photographed** if you …

_____

2. The school **auditorium** is a good place to …

_____

3. It's important to **irrigate** when …

_____

4. At a **prestigious** event you might …

_____

5. We were afraid the **inspector** would …

_____

6. The town was **impoverished** after …

_____

> Choose two of the Critical Vocabulary words and use them in a sentence.

_____

_____

_____

_____

Name _____

Text Structure

Cause and effect is a type of text structure an author uses to organize ideas in a text. An author uses cause and effect to tell the reason for an event and what happened as a result of the event.

> **Answer the questions about paragraphs 4–6 of *Winds of Hope*.**

1. What is the text structure of this part of the text, and how do you know?

_____

_____

2. How does knowing the text's structure help you understand how the relevant details support the central idea on this page?

_____

_____

> **Answer the questions about paragraphs 9 and 10 of *Winds of Hope*.**

3. What is the text structure of this part of the text?

_____

_____

4. How do you know the text structure?

_____

_____

Name _____

Long a and e

> Read each sentence. Under the blank is the phrase "long *a* sound" or "long *e* sound." Find that category of words in the box. Choose the word from that category that completes the sentence best and write it in the blank.

long *a* words	duration, holiday, afraid
long *e* words	monkey, brief, revolted, concealed, uneasy, athlete, deceive

1. Ray was _____ to go into the dark basement alone.

long *a* sound

2. I _____ the treats so that my dog won't find them.

long *e* sound

3. Keshia's favorite animal at the zoo is the _____ .

long *e* sound

4. The American colonists _____ against the British.

long *e* sound

5. Jeremy's favorite _____ is the Fourth of July.

long *a* sound

6. We had only a _____ amount of time to visit.

long *e* sound

7. I would never lie to you or try to _____ you.

long *e* sound

8. Mei was feeling _____ about the upcoming test.

long *e* sound

9. Please be quiet for the _____ of the show.

long *a* sound

10. If you practice very hard, you can become an exceptional _____ .

long *e* sound

Name _____

Critical Vocabulary

▶ Use what you know about the vocabulary words from *Wheelchair Sports: Hang Glider to Wheeler-Dealer* to help you choose which sentence best fits the meaning of the word in dark print.

1. objective

Marilyn was determined to have a full, active life.

Marilyn did not think she would ever be active again.

2. maneuver

She had a difficult time sitting in her old, heavy wheelchair.

She moved her new, light wheelchair all around the court.

3. traditional

Older, standard wheelchairs can tip easily.

Sports wheelchairs have a wide wheelbase and are very stable.

4. elite

The Paralympics are held right after the Olympics.

The best wheelchair athletes compete in the Paralympics.

5. specialized

That doctor only treated patients with spinal cord injuries.

That doctor encouraged her patients to exercise every day.

▶ Choose two of the Critical Vocabulary words and use them in a sentence.

_____

_____

_____

_____

Name _____

Central Idea

Good readers identify **central ideas** as they read to understand the text. They also look for relevant details that tell more about the central idea. Relevant details may include facts, examples, or definitions.

▶ **Answer the questions about the sidebar "Wheelchair Sports" on page 47.**

1. What is the central idea of this section of the text?

_____

_____

2. What relevant details support the central idea?

_____

_____

3. What central idea in the text does the diagram at the top of pages 48–49 support?

_____

_____

Name _____

Roots photo, aud, and vis

The word *photocopy* contains a root that has Greek origins. The meaning of the root *photo* is "light."

The word *audiologist* contains a root that has Latin origins. The meaning of the root *aud* is "hear."

The word *television* contains a root that has Latin origins. The meaning of the root *vis* is "see."

▶ **Complete the chart with other words that contain the roots *photo*, *aud*, and *vis*.**

photo	aud	vis
_____	_____	_____
_____	_____	_____
_____	_____	_____
_____	_____	_____

▶ **Choose one word from each category and use it in a sentence.**

_____

_____

_____

_____

_____

_____

_____

Name _____

Text Structure

Text structure is the way an author organizes ideas in a text. Authors use cause-and-effect text structure to show the reason for an event, and then what happened as a result of that event. Authors use chronological text structure to organize ideas in the order in which they occurred.

> Answer the questions about paragraphs 11–13 on page 50 of *Wheelchair Sports: From Hang Glider to Wheeler-Dealer*.

1. What is the text structure of this part of the text?

_____

_____

2. How do you know the text structure?

_____

_____

3. How does knowing the text's structure help you understand the central ideas of the "Guttmann's Great Idea" section?

_____

_____

_____

_____

Name _____

Long *i* and *o*

▷ At the end of each line, circle the word that contains the long *i* sound to complete the line of the poem.

1. Little bird, you fly so hey / high,

2. Way up in the sunlit sky /ski.

3. You rest upon the swaying ping / pine,

4. Where everything will be just fin / fine.

▷ At the end of each line, circle the word that contains the long *o* sound to complete the line of the poem.

5. I'm always fast, I'm never slow / slough,

6. I seldom walk or stride or stool / stroll.

7. I like to run and jump and through / throw.

8. I gallop like a horse's foal / fool.

9. I'm out in rain and sleet and how / snow.

10. I'm always, always on the go / good.

Name _____

Critical Vocabulary

You can use the words you learn from reading as you talk and write.

▶ **Use what you learned about the vocabulary words from *Captain Arsenio* to help you answer the questions below.**

1. What **impulse** does Captain Arsenio share with the Wright brothers?

_____

2. How do you know that Captain Arsenio was **passionate** about flying?

_____

3. What **circumstances** suggest that Captain Arsenio was **eccentric**?

_____

4. Which **prototype** required **acceleration** in order to work?

_____

5. Could Captain Arsenio be considered **distinguished**? Why or why not?

_____

6. **Evidently**, Captain Arsenio was injured when he tested the Flying Runner. What part of the flight diary shows this?

_____

7. What inspired Captain Arsenio to **conceive** of 18 contraptions?

_____

8. Explain whether you think Captain Arsenio made a valuable **contribution** to society.

_____

_____

▶ **Choose one Critical Vocabulary word and use it in a sentence.**

_____

Name _____

Literary Elements

The **characters** in a story are the people the story is about. The **plot** is what happens in the story. The plot contains the events of the story, or the things that happen. The plot develops around the conflict, or the main problem that characters face, which is solved in the resolution.

> **Answer the question about literary elements on page 57 of *Captain Arsenio*.**

1. What have you learned about Captain Arsenio so far? Cite evidence from the text to support your response.

   _____

   _____

   _____

> **Answer the question about literary elements on page 62 of *Captain Arsenio*.**

2. How are the Flying Runner project and Motocanary project alike?

   _____

   _____

   _____

> **Answer this additional question from page 65 about literary elements.**

3. What does the phrase "a small problem" under the sixth image in the diary entry tell you about Captain Arsenio's perspective?

   _____

   _____

   _____

Name _____

Greek Roots auto, bio; Prefixes ir-, il-

> Complete the chart with a new word that contains each of the roots or prefixes.
Write the definition for each word.

Root or Prefix	Meaning	New Word	Meaning
auto	self		
bio	life		
ir–	not		
il–	not		

> Look at each new word and its meaning. Write a sentence with each new word.

_____

_____

_____

_____

_____

_____

_____

Name _____

Author's Craft

An **author's craft** is the way that an author makes his or her writing interesting. It is how he or she uses words, sentences, and other devices to communicate ideas to the reader and to develop a writing style and the voice of a story's narrator and characters. A narrator's or character's voice can reveal his or her personality and perspective, and also help readers relate to him or her.

▶ Answer the questions about the author's craft on page 66 of *Captain Arsenio*.

1. What does the phrase "Obvious results" in paragraph 13 suggest about the narrator's perspective?

_____

_____

2. What does the scientific language in the diary entry from November 15, 1785, help you understand about Captain Arsenio's perspective?

_____

_____

▶ Answer these additional questions about the author's craft.

3. What phrases in the diary entry help you understand Captain Arsenio's perspective about success?

_____

_____

Name _____

Long *i* and *o*

▶ **Read each sentence. Find the word or words that include the long *i* or long *o* vowel sound. Underline the letter or letters that make the sound.**

1. The couple eloped, or ran away to get married.

2. At midnight, the feisty adventurers set sail over the billowing waves.

3. As fallen leaves decompose, they add richness to the soil.

4. If we amplify the sound, then everyone in the back of the room will be able to hear.

5. Three singers—a soprano, a tenor, and a bass—decided to sing together as a trio.

6. He would never knowingly break the law.

7. I tried to lift the heavy recycling bin, although I knew I couldn't.

8. The children discovered a geode among the rocks in their backyard.

9. "Please recline your seat and relax for the rest of the journey," said the pilot.

10. She put lotion with aloe on her irritated skin.

Name _____

Author's Purpose

An **author's purpose** is the reason the author chooses to write a particular text. If the author's purpose is to inform the reader, the author wants to share information about a topic. If the author's purpose is to persuade the reader, the author wants readers to think or act in a certain way. If the author's purpose is to entertain the reader, the author wants readers simply to enjoy a story or other text.

▶ **Answer the question about the author's purpose on page 60 of *Captain Arsenio*.**

1. Why do you think the author chose to include diary entries with illustrations to show each step of the Motocanary experiment?

   _____

   _____

   _____

▶ **Answer this additional question about the author's purpose.**

2. What is the author's purpose in writing this story? How do you know?

   _____

   _____

   _____

3. How do the diary images on pages 68–69 help to make the story more entertaining?

   _____

   _____

   _____

Name _____

Words with /o͞o/, /yo͞o/

▶ **Read each sentence. Find the word or words with the vowel sound /o͞o/ or /yo͞o/. Underline the letter or letters that make the sound.**

1. Dad always watches the news on TV.

2. In his youth, Shelly's grandfather played in a jazz band.

3. My sister is always asking, "Will we be there soon?"

4. I refuse to lie, so please trust that what I say is true.

5. Stew is a great food for winter.

6. If you could have any career, what would you choose?

7. "The dog ate my homework" is a weak excuse.

8. I don't know how I happened to lose so much weight, but my pants are getting loose.

Name _____

Critical Vocabulary

You can use the words you learn from reading as you talk and write.

> **Use what you learned about the vocabulary words from *Airborn* to help you finish each sentence. Then use the Critical Vocabulary words as you talk with a partner about your sentences.**

1. I began to **panic** when I found out…

_____

2. Our sailboat was far out at sea when a **favorable** wind…

_____

3. She glanced through the **porthole** and saw…

_____

4. When snow **densely** covers the yard, we can't…

_____

5. The question seems **reasonable** to me because…

_____

6. Because I was **delirious**, I couldn't…

_____

7. The image that was **projected** was…

_____

> **Now use two of the Critical Vocabulary words in a single sentence.**

_____

_____

_____

_____

Name _____

8. The **contents** of the desk included…

_____

9. One of my few **deficiencies** is…

_____

Name _____

Literary Elements

Literary elements are the pieces that make up a story. They include things such as **characters**, **plot**, **conflict**, **resolution**, and the **events** in the story.

> **Answer the questions about page 87 of** *Airborn*.

1. Where and when do events in this story take place?

_____

2. How does the setting contribute to the plot?

_____

_____

_____

> **Answer this question about page 88 and page 96 of** *Airborn*.

3. How do the early events in the journal help Matt notice a problem in the final journal entry on page 96?

_____

_____

_____

> **Answer this question about page 103 of** *Airborn*.

4. How does the dialogue hint at a resolution of the conflict in this part of the story?

_____

_____

_____

Word with /o͞o/, /yo͞o/

▶ Read each sentence. The phrase "/o͞o/ sound" or "/yo͞o/ sound" is beneath each blank line. Find the word from the box that makes the best sense in the sentence. Write the word in the blank.

/o͞o/ words	exclude, newspaper, routine, bassoon
/yo͞o/ words	interview, review, confusing, rescue

1. I am nervous about my _____ for the new job.
   /yo͞o/ sound

2. Please _____ the dying plant by watering it.
   /yo͞o/ sound

3. Ms. Yang didn't _____ anyone from the discussion.
   /o͞o/ sound

4. The directions were _____ , so I got lost.
   /yo͞o/ sound

5. The election results were reported in the _____ .
   /o͞o/ sound

6. Kendra plays the piano and the _____ .
   /o͞o/ sound

7. My morning _____ is to eat, brush my teeth, and get dressed.
   /o͞o/ sound

8. I need to _____ my notes before the quiz.
   /yo͞o/ sound

Name _____

Prefixes un–, non–, dis–; Suffixes –y, –ly/–ily

The prefixes *un–*, *non–*, and *dis–* mean "not" and are found in words such as *unreasonable*, *nonstop*, and *discovered*. The suffix *–y* is often used to turn a noun into an adjective and is found in words such as *swirly* and *windy*. The suffixes *–ly* and *–ily* are often used to turn an adjective into an adverb and are found in words such as *reasonably* and *easily*.

> Complete the chart with other words that contain the prefixes *un–*, *non–*, and *dis–* and the suffixes *–y* and *–ly/–ily*.

un–	non–	dis–
_____	_____	_____
_____	_____	_____
_____	_____	_____

–y	–ly/–ily
_____	_____
_____	_____
_____	_____

> Choose one word from each category and use it in a sentence.

_____

_____

_____

_____

_____

_____

_____

Name _____

Figurative Language

Figurative language is language used in an unexpected way to create a special effect. Examples of figurative language include **simile** (comparing two things using the word *like* or *as*), **metaphor** (comparing two things by saying one thing is or was something else), **personification** (giving human characteristics to an object or an animal), and **hyperbole** (a deliberate exaggeration).

> **Answer the questions about pages 98–99 of *Airborn*.**

1. What kinds of figurative language does the author use to describe Mount Mataurus?

_____

2. How does the author's use of figurative language add to your understanding of the setting?

_____

_____

_____

_____

_____

Name _____

Characters

A **character** is a person (or animal) in a story. Authors bring their characters to life through appearance; traits; behaviors; voice and dialogue; and perspective, thoughts, and emotions.

▶ **Answer the questions about page 90 of *Airborn*.**

1. Which character does the author develop through narration in this part of the text?

_____

2. Which character does the author develop through journal entries?

_____

3. How does the author use language to reveal each character's perspective? Cite examples from the text.

_____

_____

_____

_____

_____

_____

▶ **Answer this question about pages 99–101 of *Airborn*.**

4. How do Kate and Matt feel about Molloy? Compare and contrast their perspectives.

_____

_____

▶ **Answer the question about page 103 of *Airborn*.**

5. What do the author's words help you understand about Kate's perspective?

_____

_____

Name _____

Words with /ou/, /ô/, /oi/

▶ **Read each sentence. Find the word that has the vowel sound: /ou/, /ô/, or /oi/. Underline the letter or letters in each word that makes the vowel sound. Below the sentence, underline "/ou/ sound," "/ô/ sound," or "/oi/ sound."**

1. Ann bounced right off the trampoline!

      /ou/ sound   /ô/ sound   /oi/ sound

2. Miguel was very excited to meet the author of his favorite novel.

      /ou/ sound   /ô/ sound   /oi/ sound

3. The fans rejoiced when their team won the game.

      /ou/ sound   /ô/ sound   /oi/ sound

4. Curtis tries very hard to be loyal to his young friends.

      /ou/ sound   /ô/ sound   /oi/ sound

5. Gabriella grows beautiful flowers in her garden.

      /ou/ sound   /ô/ sound   /oi/ sound

6. My lips tasted salty after my swim in the ocean.

      /ou/ sound   /ô/ sound   /oi/ sound

7. Lance was thrilled when his plant finally began to sprout.

      /ou/ sound   /ô/ sound   /oi/ sound

8. The pioneers slept on pillows stuffed with straw.

      /ou/ sound   /ô/ sound   /oi/ sound

Name _____

Critical Vocabulary

> Use what you know about the vocabulary words from *The Secret Garden* to help you finish each sentence.

How nervous would you be if…

1. you noticed that the **fastenings** on your backpack were loose?

   _____

2. you received a **mysterious** letter in the mail?

   _____

3. after **awakening** you saw a spider on your pillow?

   _____

4. some **tendrils** appeared on your new pea plants?

   _____

5. you woke up late for school and realized that your hair was **matted**?

   _____

> Choose two of the Critical Vocabulary words and use them in a sentence.

   _____

   _____

   _____

   _____

Name _____

Literary Elements

Story structure refers to the way events in a story are organized. It is related to **plot** and **conflict**. The stages include rising action (events in the beginning of a story that create interest), climax (the part of the story where the action reaches a peak), falling action (events in the story that follow the climax), and resolution (how the conflict in a story is solved).

▶ **Answer the questions about pages 110–112 of *The Secret Garden*.**

1. What conflict or problem does Mary have after she finds the key?

_____

_____

2. In what way does the robin seem to try to help Mary?

_____

_____

3. Why doesn't Mary understand what the robin is doing at first?

_____

_____

4. How does the conflict contribute to the story?

_____

_____

5. What finally leads Mary to a resolution in the scene?

_____

_____

_____

Name _____

Words with /ou/, /ô/, /oi/

> Read each sentence. The phrase "/ou/ sound," "/ô/ sound," or "/oi/ sound" is beneath each blank line. Find the word from the box that makes the best sense in the sentence. Write the word in the blank.

/ou/ words	pronounce, scoundrel, snowplow
/ô/ words	withdrawal, astronaut, auction
/oi/ words	moisture, pointless, annoying

1. The light rain left a layer of _____ on the ground.
   /oi/ sound

2. The young child could not _____ the word *spaghetti*.
   /ou/ sound

3. Jesse made a _____ of money at the bank.
   /ô/ sound

4. That boy is a _____ who cheats on tests.
   /ou/ sound

5. The _____ was thrilled to travel to outer space.
   /ô/ sound

6. At the _____ , Michelle bid $10 for a comic book.
   /ô/ sound

7. Worrying won't help, so it's _____ .
   /oi/ sound

8. Pedro thought his little sister was _____ .
   /oi/ sound

9. A _____ just blocked our driveway.
   /ou/ sound

Name _____

Critical Vocabulary

▶ **Use what you know about the vocabulary words from** *The Miracle of Spring* **to help you answer each question.**

1. Who is **presiding** over the trial?

_____

2. What does Beaver ask his first **witness**?

_____

3. What is one problem King Bartholomew created when he **attempted** to stop spring?

_____

4. How does King Bartholomew show **contempt** of court?

_____

5. In what way does King Bartholomew have to **restrain** himself?

_____

▶ **Choose two of the Critical Vocabulary words and use them in a sentence.**

_____

_____

_____

_____

Name _____

Elements of Drama

The elements of drama are the parts of a play that give it structure and meaning. **Scenes** are similar to chapters in a story. An **act** is a section of a play that contains more than one scene. **Characters** are the people (or animals) in the play. **Dialogue** consists of the words the characters say to one another. **Setting** is where and when the story takes place. **Stage directions** tell the actors what to do and provide information about the setting. The **script** is the text of the play.

> **Answer the questions about pages 123–124 of** *The Miracle of Spring*.

1. What information do the production notes provide?

   _____

2. Which character speaks first in Act 1 of the play?

   _____

3. What line of dialogue does the character speak?

   _____

4. On page 124, what stage directions tell the king how to speak or act?

   _____

5. What do you learn about King Bartholomew's character based on his dialogue in Act 1? What kind of ruler is he?

   _____

   _____

Name _____

Prefixes *re-*, *pre-*, *post-*, and *fore-*

The prefix *re–* means "again." The prefixes *pre–* and *fore–* mean "before." The prefix *post–* means "after."

> **Complete the chart with other words that contain the prefixes *re–*, *pre–*, *post–*, and *fore–*.**

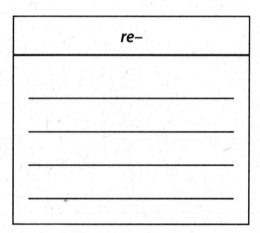

re–

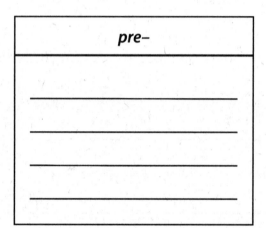

pre–

post–

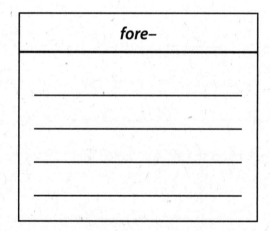

fore–

> **Choose one word from each category and use it in a sentence.**

_____

_____

_____

_____

_____

Name _____

Figurative Language

Figurative language is a rhetorical device in which language is used in an unexpected way, to create a special effect. **Personification** and **repetition** are examples of these devices. They help writers develop their characters. Figures of speech, such as **adages, proverbs,** and **puns,** add wisdom and humor to a story or play.

▶ **Answer the questions about pages 130–131 of** *The Miracle of Spring.*

1. Which character frequently uses repetition?

_____

2. How does this repetition help you understand the text?

_____

_____

3. Which characters are examples of personification in Act 2, Scene 1?

_____

▶ **Answer the questions about page 132 of** *The Miracle of Spring.*

4. What is an example of repetition the author uses in dialogue after Ms. Bee is dismissed?

_____

5. What is the author's purpose for using repetition?

_____

▶ **Answer the questions about page 136 of** *The Miracle of Spring.*

6. What pun does the king use at the end of the play?

_____

7. What does it mean?

_____

_____

8. Now write a pun of your own that one of the other characters in the play might use.

_____

Name _____

r-Controlled Vowels /ôr/, /âr/, /är/

> Read each sentence. Find the words that have the vowel sounds: "/ôr/," "/âr/," or "/är/." Underline the letters in each word that make these vowel sounds. Below the sentence, underline "/ôr/ sound," "/âr/ sound," or "/är/ sound."

1. Please be careful walking on the slippery sidewalk.

   /ôr/ sound   /âr/ sound   /är/ sound

2. Chris ordered a healthier meal than he usually does.

   /ôr/ sound   /âr/ sound   /är/ sound

3. Set your alarm for 7:30 a.m. so you have enough time to get ready.

   /ôr/ sound   /âr/ sound   /är/ sound

4. Lilla scored an 87 on yesterday's geography quiz.

   /ôr/ sound   /âr/ sound   /är/ sound

5. It was very hard to contain my excitement about the wonderful news.

   /ôr/ sound   /âr/ sound   /är/ sound

6. Go upstairs and turn off the lights.

   /ôr/ sound   /âr/ sound   /är/ sound

7. I foresee success in your future if you keep trying.

   /ôr/ sound   /âr/ sound   /är/ sound

8. Emilio received the award for most valuable player.

   /ôr/ sound   /âr/ sound   /är/ sound

Name _____

Critical Vocabulary

You can use the words you learn from reading as you talk and write.

> **Use details from *The Poem That Will Not End* to support your answers below. Then use the Critical Vocabulary words as you talk with a partner about your answers.**

Read each sentence. Make an "X" next to the sentence that best fits the meaning of the word in dark print.

hesitate ____ I wait nervously in the doorway before going inside.
____ I unlock the door and quickly go inside.

watchful ____ Our cat pays no attention to us.
____ Our cat follows us from room to room.

curse ____ There's always bad news when you talk about your bike!
____ It's much easier to get around since you got your bike!

ditty ____ Desmond sang a silly little song as he did his chores.
____ Desmond read a short story instead of doing his chores.

refrain ____ The songwriter wrote the first line of her song in an old notebook.
____ Can you remember the words she repeats in the song's chorus?

restless ____ After our long run this morning, my dog is exhausted.
____ When my dog can't sit still, I know it's time to take him out.

seized ____ A sudden hunger hit me, and all I could think about was food.
____ Delicious aromas from the kitchen had me looking forward to mealtime.

scrawled ____ Jason could barely read the handwriting on the note Kaley left him.
____ Jason carefully typed up his story just in time for class.

> **Choose one of the Critical Vocabulary words and use it in a sentence.**

_____

_____

Name _____

Elements of Poetry

Poetry looks different from other kinds of writing. The lines of a poem are shown in sections called **stanzas**. When lines in a poem **rhyme**, they end in the same or similar sounds. Poetry without rhyme is called **free verse**. **Rhythm** is a kind of beat, or meter. Certain words are stressed in each line of a poem to create a rhythm. **Imagery** is language that appeals to the reader's senses and creates images in the reader's mind.

> **Answer the questions about elements of poetry on page 143 of** *The Poem That Will Not End.*

1. Which lines rhyme in stanzas 2 and 4?

   _____

   _____

2. Read the poems "Rhythm" and "Going Bananas" that Ryan wrote. What do you notice about the rhyme pattern in "Rhythm"?

   _____

   _____

3. What do you notice about the rhyme pattern in "Going Bananas"?

   _____

   _____

   _____

4. How is the rhythm similar in both poems?

   _____

   _____

Name _____

Suffixes –ful, –less, –ment, and –ness

▷ Combine each of the following words with one or more of the suffixes from the
lesson. Use a dictionary to help you figure out which suffixes can be used for each word.
Write down the meaning of each new word you create and its part of speech.

1. care

_____

_____

2. amaze

_____

_____

3. bold

_____

_____

▷ Look at each new word and its meaning. Write a sentence with each new word.

_____

_____

_____

_____

Name _____

Author's Purpose

An **author's purpose** is the reason the author writes a particular text. If the author's purpose is to **inform** the reader, the author wants to share information about a topic. If the author's purpose is to **persuade** the reader, the author wants the reader to think or act in a certain way. If the author's purpose is to **entertain** the reader, the author wants the reader simply to enjoy a story.

> ▶ **Answer the questions about the author's purpose on page 151 of *The Poem That Will Not End.***

1. What feeling does the poet create in "Skateboard"?

   _____

   _____

2. Why do you think the poet chose to string together a series of phrases in "Skateboard" instead of breaking the poem into separate sentences?

   _____

   _____

3. Why does the poet break the lines in this way?

   _____

   _____

   _____

4. What is the author's purpose for writing this poem?

   _____

   _____

Name _____

r-Controlled Vowels /ôr/, /âr/, /är/

▶ Read each sentence. The phrase "/ôr/ sound," "/âr/ sound," or "/är/ sound" is beneath each blank line. Find the word from the box that makes the best sense in the sentence. Write the word in the blank.

/ôr/ words	restore, portrait, uproar
/âr/ words	various, prepared, despair
/är/ words	remarkable, arctic, armadillo

1. Kenji tried _____ strategies to win the game.
   /âr/ sound

2. It is _____ that the plant keeps sprouting new leaves.
   /är/ sound

3. Don't _____—you will do better next time.
   /âr/ sound

4. I can _____ the shine on this tabletop.
   /ôr/ sound

5. The artist painted a beautiful _____ of the young child.
   /ôr/ sound

6. Most people can't stay out long in the cold _____ climate.
   /är/ sound

7. Cristina was startled by the loud _____ of the crowd.
   /ôr/ sound

8. The _____ has protective armor.
   /är/ sound

9. David _____ for his test by studying hard.
   /âr/ sound

Name _____

Theme

The **theme** of a poem or other text is the main message or lesson the author wants readers to know. Sometimes an author clearly states the theme. Sometimes it's implied, or suggested, and the reader has to figure it out. A theme can be expressed in one sentence.

▶ **Answer the questions about pages 158–159 of** *The Poem That Will Not End***.**

1. Look at the illustration on page 159. How does the illustration help you understand how Ryan feels?

   _____

   _____

   _____

   _____

   _____

2. What is the lesson, or theme, the author wants to convey in this poem?

   _____

   _____

▶ **Answer this question about** *The Poem That Will Not End***.**

3. How does the title of this selection reflect its theme?

   _____

   _____

Name _____

r-Controlled Vowels /ûr/, /îr/

> Read each sentence. Find the word or words that have the *r*-controlled vowel sound you hear in *ear* or *earth*. Underline the letters that make the sound.

1. We could see the dolphin through the surface of the water.

2. My girlfriend's name is Mercy.

3. The premier is the leader of China's government.

4. The World Cup is being held in Germany next year.

5. The truck veered to avoid the car that appeared from nowhere.

6. Pedro yearned to see his brother who was away at the university.

7. The pearl necklace was the ideal purchase.

8. Shirley worked hard to put curls in her hair.

Critical Vocabulary

You can use the words you learn from reading as you talk and write.

> **Use details and ideas from** *Eruption!* **to support your answers to the questions below. Then use the Critical Vocabulary words as you talk with a partner about your answers.**

1. Why do scientists use **seismographs** when they think a volcano might erupt?

_____

_____

2. What kind of **alarming** news might lead to an **evacuation**?

_____

3. What can scientists learn from a **reservoir** of melted rock and gas under a volcano?

_____

4. What can you do to avoid falling **victim** to a natural disaster?

_____

5. If damage from a volcano is **widespread**, what **consequences** might nearby residents face?

_____

6. Why is it important for scientists to follow a volcano's progression and keep **conferring** about how to deal with it?

_____

_____

> **Choose two of the Critical Vocabulary words and use them in a sentence.**

_____

_____

Name _____

Text Structure

Text structure is the way a text is arranged to help readers understand the information. In narrative nonfiction texts, authors may use **chronological order** text structure to organize ideas.

▷ **Answer the questions about the text structure on page 178 of** *Eruption!*

1. What structure does the author use at the beginning of this text?

_____

_____

2. How do you know the author uses this text structure?

_____

_____

_____

_____

▷ **Answer this additional question about text structure.**

3. How does the author's choice of text structure help the reader understand narrative nonfiction?

_____

_____

_____

_____

Name _____

r-Controlled Vowels /ûr/, /îr/

▶ Read each sentence. Choose a word with an *r*-controlled vowel from the box that makes the best sense in the sentence. Write the word in the blank.

/ûr/ words	researcher, murky, vertical, confirm, wordy
/îr/ words	teardrop, weariness, eeriness, premiere

1. The water in the lake looked cloudy and _____ .

2. The _____ discovered a cure for the rare disease.

3. The _____ of the haunted house was scary.

4. Draw a _____ line going from top to bottom.

5. Mike watched the _____ episode of the new show.

6. Keshia called to _____ her dentist appointment for Thursday.

7. His _____ caused the tired baby to fall fast asleep.

8. She sobbed and wiped a _____ from her eye.

9. A short sentence is not very _____ .

Name _____

Greek Roots graph/gram; Latin Roots rupt, fer

The words *seismograph*, *eruption*, and *conferring* contain roots that have Greek or Latin origins. The meaning of the Greek root *graph* or *gram* is "written, drawn, or recorded." The meaning of the Latin root *rupt* is "break or burst," and the meaning of the Latin root *fer* is "carry or bring."

> **Complete the chart with other words that contain the roots *graph*, *gram*, *rupt*, and *fer*.**

graph	gram
_____	_____
_____	_____
_____	_____
rupt	**fer**
_____	_____
_____	_____
_____	_____

> **Choose one word from each category and use it in a sentence.**

_____

_____

_____

_____

_____

_____

Name _____

Figurative Language

Authors use **imagery** to make their writing clear and engaging. Imagery uses **sensory words** that convey how something looks, tastes, feels, sounds, or smells. This helps readers feel "like they are there" in a story.

> **Answer the question about the figurative language on page 182 of** *Eruption!*

1. What sensory words and phrases help you visualize the evacuation?

_____

_____

_____

_____

_____

> **Answer this additional question about the figurative language on page 184.**

2. What are some sensory words and phrases that help you understand the action on the page?

_____

_____

_____

_____

_____

Name _____

Content-Area Words

Content-area words are words used in a text that are specific to a subject, such as math, science, or social studies. Readers can use **context clues** and their knowledge of word roots to help them determine the meaning of content-area words. Readers can also use **dictionaries** to check the meaning.

> **Answer these questions about page 179 of** *Eruption!*

1. What are some content-area words in paragraph 7 of *Eruption!*?

_____

_____

_____

2. What might help you understand their meanings?

_____

_____

_____

> **Answer this additional question about content-area words.**

3. What other resources can you use to understand content-area words?

_____

_____

_____

Name _____

Compound Words

▶ Read each sentence. Choose the compound word from the box that best completes each sentence, and write it in the blank.

fireflies	raincoat	sandcastle	motorcycle	seashore
afternoon	anyone	airplanes	saucepan	homemade

1. It was great fun to watch the _____ take off and land.

2. Dave needed a new _____ as his got burned the last time he cooked in it.

3. The roaring _____ disrupted the quiet of the country road.

4. What time will the soccer game start this _____ ?

5. On that stormy day, I wore my _____ and took my umbrella.

6. One of Joaquín's baking specialties is _____ brownies.

7. Does _____ know the answer to question number 6?

8. I like to catch _____ on summer evenings.

9. The children spent most of the day digging a giant hole at the _____ .

10. After they dug the giant hole, the children built a _____ .

Name _____

Critical Vocabulary

▶ Use what you know about the vocabulary words from *Alaska Earthquakes* to help you answer each question.

How would you feel if…

1. you realized that **prior** to leaving the house, you had put on two different shoes?

_____

2. you **literally** had only one dollar for lunch?

_____

3. the **magnitude** of your school project was more than you could handle completing alone?

_____

4. you forgot to do **maintenance** on your bike before setting off on a long ride?

_____

▶ Choose two of the Critical Vocabulary words and use them in a sentence.

_____

_____

_____

_____

Name _____

Media Techniques

Media is the term used to include all the ways in which ideas can be communicated to an audience. **Media techniques**, which include visual and sound elements, are tools media creators use to get their messages across to audiences effectively.

▶ **Answer the questions about the audio and visual elements in** *Between the Glacier and the Sea: The Alaska Earthquake.*

1. How does the video describe the sounds of an earthquake?

_____

_____

_____

_____

2. Which images best show what happens when there is an earthquake?

_____

_____

_____

_____

3. How do images and narration work together in the video to explain earthquakes?

_____

_____

_____

_____

Name _____

Compound Words

> Read each sentence. Choose the word from the box that best completes each sentence, and write it in the blank.

carpool	merry-go-round	waterproof	fingernails	grandchildren
washcloth	sunshine	flashlight	playground	credit card

1. My _____ were dirty after I pulled weeds in the garden.

2. Go outside and play in the fresh air and _____ .

3. Ms. Mathers drives the _____ on Mondays.

4. Mr. Reyes likes to take his _____ to the zoo.

5. The girls played basketball on the _____ after school.

6. Sarah took a ride on the _____ at the county fair.

7. My mother paid for dinner with a _____ .

8. Mason was glad his watch was _____ after he fell in the pool.

9. Scrub your face with a _____ before you go to bed.

10. Luisa carried a _____ down into the dark basement.

Name _____

Critical Vocabulary

▶ Underline the sentence that best fits the meaning of the word in dark print. Use what you know about the vocabulary words from *Quaking Ground, Racing Waves* to help you.

1. destruction

The mayor urged everyone to leave town.

The tornado ripped through town and flattened almost every home.

2. triggered

The smoke from the broiled fish set off the smoke detector.

Clouds of black smoke rose from the factory.

3. thrust

Ruth couldn't help smiling when she heard the applause.

Her fellow cast members pushed Ruth back into the spotlight.

4. radiate

Wind blew through the cracked, drafty windows.

The warmth from the heater will spread to the whole room.

5. parallel

You can turn left from Maple Avenue onto Elm Street.

Elm Street and Maple Avenue run east to west one block apart.

6. lateral

The dancers' movements were full of energy and rhythm.

The dance instructor told the line of dancers to shift to the right.

7. modified

I used olive oil instead of butter to make these muffins.

I forgot to set the timer, so the first set of muffins burned.

> **Choose two of the Critical Vocabulary words and use them in a sentence.**

_____

_____

_____

Name _____

Author's Craft

An **author's craft** is the way that an author makes his or her writing interesting. It is how he or she communicates ideas to the reader. Part of an author's craft is the author's **voice**. This refers to his or her individual writing style. It is what makes the writing unique. An author's voice can be funny or serious, formal or informal. Word choice helps to create an author's voice.

> **Answer these questions about author's craft on page 203 of** *Quaking Earth, Racing Waves*.

1. What comparison does the author use to help readers understand that the lithosphere is very thin?

_____

_____

_____

_____

2. How does the author explain how slowly Earth's plates move?

_____

_____

_____

_____

3. What vivid verbs does the author use to help readers visualize the way Earth's plates move?

_____

_____

_____

_____

Name _____

Root *geo*; Suffixes *–logy* and *–logist*

The word *geography* contains a root that has Greek origins. The meaning of the root *geo* is "earth."

The suffix *–logy* means "the study of" and *–logist* means "one who does."

> Complete the chart with other words that contain the root *geo* and the suffixes *–logy* and *–logist*.

geo	*–logy*	*–logist*
_____	_____	_____
_____	_____	_____
_____	_____	_____

> Choose one word from each category and use it in a sentence.

_____

_____

_____

_____

Name _____

Central Idea

The **central idea** is what a text is mostly about. In some informational texts, authors divide the text into sections that give information about specific aspects of the topic. In each section, relevant details—such as facts, examples, statistics, and definitions—tell more about the central idea of that section. Taken together, the central ideas of the sections support the central idea of the entire text.

> **Answer these questions about the central idea on page 204 of *Quaking Earth, Racing Waves*.**

1. What is this section about?

_____

_____

_____

_____

2. What is the central idea of this section?

_____

_____

_____

_____

VCCV Syllable Division Pattern

▶ **Read each sentence. In its underlined VCCV word, draw a line to divide the word into syllables.**

1. I don't like rainstorms, but I love <u>blizzards</u>.

2. Jolee cut down several trees and sold the <u>lumber</u>.

3. Ms. Wu doesn't usually <u>assign</u> too much homework.

4. Annika slept poorly and woke up feeling <u>sluggish</u>.

5. The <u>concept</u> of the movie is very interesting.

6. Declan writes in his <u>journal</u> every day.

7. It's time to <u>harvest</u> all of these vegetables.

8. My favorite season of the year is <u>summer</u>.

Critical Vocabulary

You can use the words you learn from reading as you talk and write.

> Use what you learned about the vocabulary words from *Hurricanes: The Science Behind Killer Storms* to help you finish each sentence.

1. One of the warmest regions on Earth is _____

2. Scientists track animals in the wild to _____

3. Make sure the store's sign is anchored because _____

4. I grouped these books in the same category because _____

5. A mobile library is one that _____

6. Eventually hurricane winds _____

7. During a storm, a surge of water _____

> Choose two of the Critical Vocabulary words and use them in original sentences.

_____

_____

_____

_____

_____

_____

_____

_____

Name _____

Text and Graphic Features

Text and graphic features are visual pieces of information included in a text. **Text features** include headings and boldfaced words. **Graphic features** include illustrations and diagrams. An author uses text and graphic features to help explain information.

▶ **Answer the questions about the map on page 217 of** *Hurricanes: The Science Behind Killer Storms.*

1. What does this map show?

_____

_____

2. How does the map help you understand the text?

_____

_____

_____

▶ **Answer this question about text features using the sidebar on page 218.**

3. How does information in this section connect to ideas in the main text?

_____

_____

_____

▶ **Answer this question about the graphic feature on page 225.**

4. What information does the chart provide?

_____

_____

_____

Name _____

Prefixes inter-, com-, con-, cor-

> Review the meanings of the prefixes *inter-*, *com-*, *con-*, *cor-*. Complete the chart by finding one word that begins with each prefix. Use a dictionary or online resource to come up with words you do not know. Next to each word, write its definition.

Prefix	Word and definition
inter–	
com–	
con–	
cor–	

> Write a sentence for each word in the chart.

_____

_____

_____

_____

_____

_____

_____

_____

_____

_____

_____

_____

_____

Name _____

Content-Area Words

Content-area words are words that are specific to a particular **domain**, or area of study. An author uses content-area words to help explain information. Readers use **context clues** to help determine the meaning of unfamiliar content-area words.

▶ **Answer the questions about paragraphs 8–10 on page 216 of** *Hurricanes: The Science Behind Killer Storms.*

1. What clues help you understand the meaning of *eye* in the phrase "eye of the storm"?

   _____

   _____

2. Which phrase helps you understand what an *eyewall* is?

   _____

   _____

▶ **Answer another question about content-area words in** *Hurricanes: The Science Behind Killer Storms.*

3. How does the author's use of scientific and weather-related words and phrases affect your reading of this text?

   _____

   _____

   _____

   _____

   _____

Name _____

VCCV Syllable Division Pattern

▶ **For each sentence, find a word in the box that has a VCCV syllable division pattern and completes the sentence in a way that makes sense. Write it on the blank line. Not every word in the box has a VCCV syllable division pattern.**

boiling	city	flakes	flurries	former
previous	marina	husband	mirror	boiling
pillars	molten	rushed	urban	harbor

1. Sawyer learned about hot, _____ lava in geology class.

2. Jazmin prefers living in an area that is _____, not in the country.

3. Abdul checked his hair in the _____ before he left home.

4. Eden and her _____ have been married for six years.

5. The snow _____ looked beautiful floating down from the sky.

6. Captain Jones anchored her boat in a quiet _____ .

7. Omari's _____ home was in a large apartment building, but now he lives in a small house near the beach.

8. The porch roof is supported by four _____ .

Text Structure

Cause and effect is a type of **text structure** an author uses to organize ideas in a text. An author uses cause-and-effect structure to explain what happened and why it happened.

> **Answer the questions about the section "Heavy Rains" on page 223 of** *Hurricanes: The Science Behind Killer Storms.*

1. What text structure is used in this section?

_____

_____

2. How can you tell?

_____

_____

_____

_____

> **Answer another question about text structure in** *Hurricanes: The Science Behind Killer Storms.*

3. What does the cause-and-effect text structure in this text help you understand about hurricanes? Explain.

_____

_____

_____

_____

_____

VCV Syllable Division Pattern

> Read each sentence. The underlined word in each sentence has a VCV syllable pattern. Draw a line between the letters where the syllables are divided.

1. Make sure you exert pressure on the cut so it will stop bleeding.

2. Please omit your name from your voting ballot.

3. Steve found the nail wedged in a crevice of the cabinet.

4. A decade is ten years.

5. Sanjeet played Minor League Baseball.

6. The heroic firefighter was given a medal for bravery.

7. This is going to be a superb party.

8. The snow finally began to taper off late in the afternoon.

Name _____

Critical Vocabulary

You can use the words you learn from reading as you talk and write.

▶ **Use what you learned about the vocabulary words from** *Explore the Wild West!* **to help you finish each sentence. Then use the Critical Vocabulary words as you talk with a partner about your sentences.**

1. I have no **knowledge** of . . .

_____

2. One way that **posts** were useful to pioneers was . . .

_____

3. I think one of the greatest **hardships** is . . .

_____

4. My favorite **slogans** are . . .

_____

5. My **typical** breakfast is . . .

_____

6. Our weekend **consisted** of . . .

_____

7. One thing that it is **handy** to have in your home is . . .

_____

8. One way that people show that they are **patriotic** is by . . .

_____

▶ **Choose two of the Critical Vocabulary words and use them in a sentence.**

_____

_____

Name _____

Central Idea

The **central idea** of a selection is the big idea or the main point the writer wants readers to understand. You will find **relevant details** throughout the selection that explain or expand on the central idea.

▶ **Answer these questions about the central idea on page 248 of** *Explore the Wild West!*

1. What is the central idea of the paragraph "Presenting . . . James Beckwourth"?

_____

_____

_____

2. What relevant details support the central idea?

_____

_____

_____

▶ **Answer these questions about the central idea on pages 249–250 of** *Explore the Wild West!*

3. What is the central idea of the "Moving West" section?

_____

_____

4. What relevant details and evidence support the central idea?

_____

_____

_____

_____

VCV Syllable Division Pattern

> Read each sentence. For each sentence, select the word from the box that makes the most sense in the sentence. Then, draw a line between the two syllables.

talent	cousin	bonus	camel
humid	laser	music	miser

1. The superhero used a _____ beam to defeat the monster.

2. Craig's _____ took him on a camping trip.

3. The winner of the contest received a _____ .

4. The greedy _____ won't share any of his wealth.

5. Milagros has a great deal of artistic _____ .

6. Tom loved listening to all the new _____ .

7. The weather is very hot and _____ .

8. A _____ can go for weeks without drinking any water.

Name _____

Prefix mid-; Suffixes -al, -ic; Greek Roots homo, hetero

The prefix *mid–* means "in the middle" and is found in words such as *midland* and *midday*. The suffixes *–al* and *–ic* mean "having to do with, relating to, or having the characteristics of" and are found in words such as *natural* and *patriotic*. The Greek root *homo* means "the same" and *hetero* means "different."

▶ **Complete the chart with other words that contain the prefix *mid–*, the suffixes *–al* and *–ic*, and the Greek roots *homo* and *hetero*.**

mid–	–al	–ic
_____	_____	_____
_____	_____	_____
_____	_____	_____
homo	**hetero**	
_____	_____	
_____	_____	
_____	_____	

▶ **Choose one word from each category and use it in a sentence.**

_____

_____

_____

_____

_____

_____

Name _____

Text Structure

Informational texts are structured, or arranged, to help readers understand the information. Authors use a **problem/solution** structure to show how to solve a problem.

> **Answer the questions about text structure on page 251 of *Explore the Wild West!***

1. What problems did the pioneers face?

_____

_____

_____

_____

2. What solutions did they devise to solve these problems?

_____

_____

_____

> **Answer this additional question about text structure.**

3. How does text structure help you understand this text?

_____

_____

_____

_____

_____

Name _____

Author's Craft

Tone is the author's attitude toward a subject. A tone can be serious, humorous, sarcastic, sad, etc. **Voice** is the author's style, length of sentences, and way of writing.

▶ **Answer the question about author's craft on pages 252–253 of *Explore the Wild West!***

1. What is the author's tone and voice in the selection?

_____

_____

_____

▶ **Answer this additional question about author's craft.**

2. How do the author's tone and voice help you understand this selection?

_____

_____

_____

_____

_____

VCCCV Syllable Division Pattern

> **Read each sentence. Find the word in the sentence that has the VCCCV syllable division pattern and underline it. Then draw a line between the two syllables.**

1. There are one hundred days left in the school year.

2. You can improve your guitar skills by practicing.

3. They resolved their conflict and are now friends.

4. Sue and John walked farther than Rafael did.

5. Ranjeet was excited to pick oranges in the orchard.

6. Seth and Sulita are partners for the science project.

7. The auditorium filled with the sound of laughter.

8. The kids usually complain during long car trips.

Critical Vocabulary

> Use what you know about the vocabulary words from *The Celestials' Railroad* to help you answer each question.

How excited would you be if…

1. no one thanked you for making a **sacrifice**?

_____

2. you were **employed** to do something that you really liked?

_____

3. you heard a **complaint** about something you worked hard on?

_____

4. you saw a **celestial** event?

_____

> Choose two of the Critical Vocabulary words and use them in a sentence.

_____

_____

_____

_____

Name _____

Central Idea

Readers can identify **central ideas** as they read to understand the text. Sometimes the central idea is stated directly. Other times it is implied, and readers must infer the central idea based on text **evidence**.

> **Answer the question about pages 262–263 of *The Celestials' Railroad*.**

1. What is the central idea on these two pages?

_____

_____

_____

_____

> **Answer the questions about the sidebar text, "Come One, Come All," on page 266.**

2. What is the central idea of this paragraph?

_____

_____

_____

_____

_____

_____

3. What relevant details support this central idea?

_____

_____

_____

_____

Name _____

VCCCV Syllable Division Pattern

▶ Read each sentence. Fill in the blank with a word from the box that makes the most sense in the sentence. Then, draw a line between the two syllables in the word.

sandwich	Congress	single	complete
sample	childhood	distrust	contract

1. The man reflected on his _____ as he celebrated his 90th birthday.

2. Paul decided to make a _____ with all the Thanksgiving leftovers.

3. She hasn't given us any reason to _____ her.

4. Juan signed a _____ before he started his new job.

5. _____ is responsible for making bills into laws.

6. Tom didn't catch a _____ fish.

7. Charlie took a _____ of the seasonal flavor, pumpkin spice.

8. Please sit quietly once you _____ the assignment.

Name _____

Critical Vocabulary

▶ **Underline the sentence that best fits the meaning of the word in dark print. Use what you know about the vocabulary words from *Homesteading* to help you.**

1. domain

The queen ruled over a large area of land.

The queen wanted to help as many people as she could.

2. ideology

Abraham Lincoln served as president during the Civil War.

Abraham Lincoln believed that owning land was important.

3. primary

I have one important reason for saving money.

I have reasons for saving money.

4. residence

This is the place where I work.

This is the place where I live.

5. homestead

My great-grandfather moved to California to look for gold.

My great-grandfather moved to the Midwest to become a farmer.

▶ **Choose two of the Critical Vocabulary words and use them in a sentence.**

_____

_____

_____

_____

Name _____

Text Structure

Writers of texts and videos choose to organize their ideas and information in a structure that helps them communicate their ideas. In a historical text or video, the writer might use a **cause-and-effect** structure to explain what happened and why it happened.

▶ **Answer the questions about cause and effect in *Homesteading*.**

1. What attracted the homesteaders to the new land?

_____

_____

_____

_____

2. Why was the land free?

_____

_____

_____

_____

Name _____

Prefix trans–; Suffixes -ous, –ious; Latin Root circum

The word **transcontinental** has the prefix **trans–**, which means "across." The words **disastrous** and **victorious** contain the suffixes **–ous** and **–ious**, which mean "full of." The Latin root **circum** means "around."

▶ Complete the chart with other words that contain the prefix *trans–*, the suffixes *–ous* and *–ious*, and the Latin root *circum*.

trans–	–ous	–ious	circum
_____	_____	_____	_____
_____	_____	_____	_____
_____	_____	_____	_____

▶ Choose one word from each category and use it in a sentence.

_____

_____

_____

_____

_____

_____

_____

_____

_____

Name _____

Media Techniques

Media techniques are the ways in which ideas are communicated to viewers. Media techniques include visual and sound elements. They help viewers better understand the information presented in **media**.

▶ Answer the questions about how the narration is tied to the visuals in *Homesteading*.

1. What does the narration tell you about the Dakota Territory?

_____

_____

_____

_____

2. What do you learn about the Dakota Territory from the visuals?

_____

_____

_____

_____

3. How are J.G. Towle's letter and the narrator's account at the beginning of the video alike and different?

_____

_____

_____

_____

Name _____

VV Syllable Division Pattern

> Underline the word with the VV syllable division pattern that completes each sentence.

1. Claire was thirsty, so she drank some _____ .

juice   fluid

2. Gabriel dreamed of traveling to _____ one day.

India   Russia

3. If you're having trouble with your device, check the _____ .

manual   instructions

4. The violinist and the cellist played a _____ together.

piece   duet

5. Abdullah decided that his favorite subject is _____ .

reading   science

6. Ms. Kim assigned a project on African American _____ .

poetry   food

7. I learned about the big news on the _____ .

television   radio

8. The store offered low prices on appliances like _____ .

dryers   toasters

Name _____

Critical Vocabulary

▶ **You can use the words you learn from reading as you talk and write. Use details and ideas from** *A Pioneer Sampler* **to support your answers to the questions below.**

1. What does it look like when the oxen begin their **plod**?

_____

2. Why isn't Willy worried about clouds that look **dainty**?

_____

3. Why do farmers keep crops in a barn until they **thresh** it?

_____

4. How might Willy's voice have sounded when he **regaled** his uncle with his story about the oxen?

_____

5. Why does the author say that Willy's story with the oxen grew to "heroic **proportions**"?

_____

6. Why are **frolics** important to the Robertsons as they harvest their crops?

_____

7. What problem does the grass **stubble** create for Willy when he brings water to the fields?

_____

8. Why did Willy get upset when George acted like he was **indispensable**?

_____

9. What made Pa and George less **oblivious** as they worked on the haystack?

_____

▶ **Choose two of the Critical Vocabulary words and use them in a sentence.**

_____

Name _____

Literary Elements

Literary elements are all the pieces that make up a story. This includes the **characters**, or the people in the story. Readers discover what characters are like by what they think, do, and say. Another key element in a story is the **setting**, the time and place in which a story happens.

▶ **Answer the question about literary elements on page 281 of *A Pioneer Sampler*.**

1. What do Willy's thoughts and actions tell you about his perspective toward George's behavior?

_____

_____

_____

_____

_____

▶ **Answer this additional question about literary elements on page 283.**

2. How does the setting affect Willy's character development?

_____

_____

_____

_____

Name _____

Prefixes *mis–/mal–*, Suffixes *–able/–ible*

▶ Complete the chart by predicting the meaning of each word using your knowledge of the prefixes and suffixes to help you. Then use a print or online dictionary to confirm your prediction.

Word	I think it means. . .	Dictionary definition
mishap		
malcontent		
advisable		
convertible		

▶ Write a sentence for each word in the chart.

_____

_____

_____

_____

_____

_____

_____

Name _____

Point of View

Point of view refers to who tells a story, or the narrator of that story. A first-person narrator is part of the story, and refers to himself or herself with the pronouns *I* or *me*. A third-person narrator is someone outside of the story who uses pronouns like *he* or *she* to refer to all the characters.

▶ **Answer the questions about point of view on pages 278–279 of *A Pioneer Sampler*.**

1. What is the point of view on these pages? Who is the narrator? How do you know?

_____

_____

_____

_____

_____

_____

_____

▶ **Answer these additional questions about point of view on pages 280–281.**

2. How has the point of view shifted?

_____

_____

_____

_____

3. How does this point of view help you understand the characters?

_____

_____

Name _____

VV Syllable Division Pattern

> On each line, underline the word with the VV syllable division pattern.

1. Australia   Canada   Greece

2. repeat   react   retreat

3. genuine   real   authentic

4. straight   stream   science

5. dial   death   dream

6. menu   medium   monstrous

7. poetry   people   piece

8. tried   trail   trial

Name _____

Varieties of English

Varieties of English refers to the different ways we speak and write, depending upon our audience. We use **informal language** when we are speaking to our friends and family. Characters in a story might also use informal language when they are speaking. When we use **formal language**, we are usually speaking to someone official or writing something important. Formal language does not use slang or colorful expressions, and the words are more precise.

▶ **Answer the question about varieties of English on page 284 of** *A Pioneer Sampler.*

1. What are some examples of dialect on the page?

_____

_____

_____

_____

▶ **Answer this additional question about varieties of English.**

2. Why do you think the author chose to use informal language for Uncle Jacob?

_____

_____

_____

_____

Name _____

Final Stable Syllables -*al*, -*el*, -*le*, -*il*

▶ **Choose a word from the box with the correct final stable syllable to complete each sentence. Write the word on the blank.**

cradle	fiddle	sample	pretzel	dismissal
basil	tunnel	naval	gravel	cable

Words with -*el*

1. The train emerged from the _____ into the bright sunlight.

2. Ari bought a hot _____ with mustard from the cart at the corner.

3. The workers spread fresh _____ over the driveway.

Words with -*le*

4. The baby napped peacefully in his _____ .

5. Annika liked to _____ different kinds of bread at the bakery.

6. Steven's favorite part of the concert was the _____ music.

7. Mike needs a new _____ to connect his video game system.

Words with -*al* and -*il*

8. Rafael used _____ from his garden in his tomato sauce.

9. The ships took part in a gigantic _____ battle.

10. _____ from school was at 1:00 today because of bad weather.

Critical Vocabulary

You can use the words you learn from reading as you talk and write.

> ▷ Use details and ideas from *Potatoes on Rooftops* to support your answers to the questions below. Then use the Critical Vocabulary as you talk with a partner about your sentences.

1. Why is it difficult to have a garden in an **urban** area?

_____

2. What is one way to **transform** an outdoor area?

_____

3. What would make you describe a garden as **humble**?

_____

4. When is it useful to have **artificial** lighting as an **alternative** to sunlight?

_____

5. When might a farmer be happy with her **yield**?

_____

6. How did the two World Wars **influence** food production?

_____

_____

7. What could a family do with three or four small **plots**?

_____

> ▷ Choose two of the Critical Vocabulary words and use them in a sentence.

_____

_____

Name _____

Author's Purpose

An **author's purpose** is his or her reason for writing a text. If the author's purpose is to persuade, the writer wants readers to think or act in a certain way. If the author's purpose is to inform, the writer wants to share information about a topic. Writers of persuasive texts often target a certain audience or try to reach a certain group of readers. Who an author is addressing can affect how he or she phrases a claim or presents evidence.

> **Answer the questions about pages 308–311 of *Potatoes on Rooftops.***

1. What is this section mainly about?

_____

_____

2. What is the author's perspective about these types of gardens?

_____

_____

3. What facts does the author provide to support her claim?

_____

_____

> **Now answer these additional questions about the author's purpose from page 314.**

4. What is the author's perspective in this section?

_____

_____

5. What is her purpose for including it?

_____

_____

Name _____

Final Stable Syllables –al, –el, –le, –il

> Read each sentence, then read the two words below the sentence. Choose the word with the –al, –el, –le, or –il ending, and write it in the blank to complete the sentence.

1. Christy enjoyed reading the _____ story.

                 fictional   *nonfiction*

2. This flu is making me feel _____ .

                 sickly   *miserable*

3. The snowy woods at night were quiet and _____ .

                 peaceful   *tranquil*

4. After a long run, Cameron iced his sore _____ .

                 tendon   *muscle*

5. You can only control yourself, not _____ factors.

                 external   *outside*

6. Angela learned to ride a _____ when she was three years old.

                 scooter   *tricycle*

7. Dr. Sykes wears _____ eyeglasses.

                 bifocal   *prescription*

8. I added a _____ to each part of the diagram.

                 caption   *label*

Name ____________________

Suffix –ive

The suffix *–ive* means "tending to" or "having the nature of" and is found in words such as ***alternative*** and ***explosive***.

Complete the chart with other words that end with the suffix *–ive*.

–ive

Write a sentence for each word in the chart.

Name _____

Ideas and Support

In a persuasive text, authors try to persuade or influence readers to think a certain way. The author states a **claim** and supports that claim as part of an **argument**. Readers must decide if the author is stating a **fact** or giving an **opinion** to support the claim. A fact is something that can be proven. Clues in the text that indicate something is a fact include numbers, photos, maps, and eye-witness reports. An opinion is a personal belief; it cannot be proven true.

▶ **Answer the questions about pages 312–317 of _Potatoes on Rooftops_.**

1. What is the author's claim about urban gardens?

_____

_____

2. How does evidence in the "Digging In" section support the author's claim?

_____

_____

3. Does the author mainly use facts or opinions to support her reasoning?

_____

4. How do you know?

_____

_____

_____

5. What opinion does the author present in "Good Eats"?

_____

6. How does the author support this claim?

_____

Name _____

Author's Craft

Author's craft is the language and techniques writers use to make their writing interesting and to communicate ideas. Sometimes these techniques are called rhetorical devices. Three examples are **anecdote** (a short, funny, or interesting story that illustrates a point), **hyperbole** (exaggeration that makes things sound bigger, better, worse, or more than what they truly are), and **stereotype** (a widely believed, but often untrue, idea about a culture or group of people).

▷ **Answer the questions about pages 304–305 of *Potatoes on Rooftops*.**

1. How is the author using exaggeration to appeal to readers' emotions?

_____

_____

_____

_____

_____

_____

2. How does the sidebar "A Taste of Freedom" show the author's perspective? Use evidence from the text to support your response.

_____

_____

_____

_____

_____

▷ **Answer the question from page 312.**

3. What does the idiom "digging in" mean?

_____

_____

Name _____

Recognize Root Words

> Read each sentence. Find the word with a suffix and underline the root word.

1. The whole class went to see the magician's show.

2. You can pay for your selection at the front of the store.

3. What is the weather prediction for tomorrow?

4. I did not hear the doorbell because I was listening to music.

5. Chris went into the yard and discovered a wild bear!

6. The very clean restaurant will pass the inspection.

7. The musician could play the violin, piano, and flute.

8. Mia cast her vote in the school board election.

Name _____

Critical Vocabulary

> Underline the sentence that best fits the meaning of the word in dark print. Use what you know about the vocabulary words from *Living Green* to help you.

1. implying

You'll be surprised how nice it is to have a clean room.

You must clean your room before you go outside.

2. cascading

The mist from the river surrounded us in the early morning.

A river flowed alongside the bike trail.

3. depleted

Is our supply of paper almost gone?

Can we keep our supply of paper on this shelf?

4. reduce

Add a sprinkle of salt to improve the flavor.

Try to use less salt on the food you eat.

5. contradict

Do exactly what I say and do!

Do what I say, not what I do!

6. conscious

Lavonne was lost in thought as she walked through the forest.

Lavonne was aware of every sound as she walked through the forest.

> Choose two of the Critical Vocabulary words and use them in a sentence.

_____

Name _____

Elements of Drama

A play, or **drama**, is a story that can be performed for an audience. The format or structure of a drama has elements that are different from other kinds of stories. The **cast of characters** is the list at the beginning of a play that names each character. A **scene** is a section of a play. Lines of dialogue are the words that actors say to each other. The **stage directions** are the instructions that tell how the actors should move or speak. They also identify the **setting** for each scene. They also may describe the appearance of the stage, lighting, or sound effects.

> **Answer these questions about elements of drama on page 324 of** *Living Green*.

1. What information does the author share before the play begins? What is the purpose of this part of the play?

   _____

   _____

   _____

2. In the first few lines of the play, what information is given in parentheses after the characters' names? Why is this information important?

   _____

   _____

   _____

   _____

3. How does the dialogue between Grace and Bo present a conflict?

   _____

   _____

   _____

   _____

Name _____

Recognize Root Words

▶ **Read each sentence. Choose the root word from the box that best completes each sentence. Write the word in the blank.**

refresh	guard	elect	collect
confess	detect	invent	reflect

1. When you admit to doing something wrong, you are making a _____ion.

2. I saw my _____ion in the mirror.

3. Keisha _____ed a clue that solved the mystery.

4. The engineer's _____ion was an automobile that ran on solar power.

5. Drinking lemonade on a very hot day is so _____ing.

6. Most adults voted in the last presidential _____ion.

7. I have a _____ion of over 50 baseball cards.

8. Everyone must have this form signed by a parent or _____ian.

Critical Vocabulary

▷ Use what you know about the vocabulary words from *The Good Garden* to help you answer each question.

How happy would you be if...

1. you found a **packet** of seeds?

_____

2. a barking dog started to **retreat**?

_____

3. you were part of a **spectacle** on the playground?

_____

4. a child **toddling** toward you suddenly fell?

_____

▷ Choose two of the Critical Vocabulary words and use them in a sentence.

_____

_____

_____

_____

Name _____

Literary Elements

Literary elements are the parts that make up the story. These include the characters, or the people in the story, and the **plot**, or what happens in the story. The plot of a story is made up of the main problem, or conflict, and the **events** that tell what happens to solve it. Each event in a story builds on the one before it, as characters try different ways to solve the problem. In this way, the events lead to a solution, or resolution, of the conflict.

▷ **Answer these questions about literary elements on page 332 of *The Good Garden*.**

1. What surprise do María Luz and her classmates encounter at school?

_____

_____

2. How do Don Pedro and his "big ideas" affect the plot?

_____

_____

_____

_____

▷ **Answer this additional question about literary elements.**

3. What is the main problem that María Luz has?

_____

_____

_____

Name _____

Latin Roots dict, spect

The word *contradict* contains a root that has Latin origins. The meaning of the root *dict* is "say." The word *spectacle* contains a root that has Latin origins. The meaning of the root *spect* is "see."

▶ Complete the chart with other words that contain the roots *dict* and *spect*.

dict	*spect*
_____	_____
_____	_____
_____	_____

▶ Choose one word from each category and use it in a sentence.

_____

_____

_____

_____

_____

_____

Name _____

Figurative Language

Authors use various types of **figurative language** to show connections between things and ideas and to enhance their storytelling. Figurative language engages the readers' imagination, feelings, and senses, and allows them to form a stronger connection to what they read. **Imagery** describes words that appeal to the readers' senses. When a writer uses imagery, he or she wants to help the readers create pictures in their minds so they can feel what the characters feel.

> ▶ **Answer these questions about figurative language on page 332 of *The Good Garden*.**

1. Which words or phrases help you picture María Luz's walk to school?

_____

_____

_____

_____

2. What kind of atmosphere, or mood, do these images create?

_____

_____

_____

> ▶ **Answer this additional question about figurative language on page 339.**

3. What words and phrases help you picture how María Luz feels during her encounter with Señor Lobo?

_____

_____

_____

Name _____

Recognize Root Words with Spelling Changes

▷ **Read each sentence or pair of sentences. Read the word in bold type. Then complete the sentence with the correct root word of the word in bold type.**

1. Children may have trouble **sharing** toys. They need to learn to _____ .

2. Liz **whined** a lot when she was little, but now knows not to _____ .

3. People use many **coping** strategies to _____ with difficult situations.

4. After Rey saw the bicyclists **riding**, he wanted to learn to _____ a bicycle, too.

5. When **choosing** a new jacket, be sure to _____ one that will keep you warm in cold weather.

6. The manager **hired** several new employees this month and will _____ more next month.

7. After **slicing** her finger, Luisa decided not to _____ more vegetables.

8. He **braved** the blizzard to go buy groceries, but he refused to _____ it again to buy candy.

Name _____

Critical Vocabulary

You can use the words you learn from reading as you talk and write.

▶ **Use what you learned about the vocabulary words from *Parrots Over Puerto Rico* to help you finish each sentence.**

1. A movie superhero who has the power of **flight** can _____

2. We guessed the boat was a **merchant** ship because _____

3. The soldiers stayed in their **fort** because _____

4. **Jabbing** at that thin wall will probably _____

5. Someone in **captivity** hopes _____

6. An **aggressive** animal may _____

7. A person who is forced to **toil** under the hot sun may _____

▶ **Choose two of the Critical Vocabulary words and use them in a sentence.**

_____

_____

_____

_____

_____

_____

Name _____

Text Structure

Problem/Solution is a type of **text structure** an author uses to organize ideas in a text. An author uses problem/solution to explain a problem and how it is, or can be, solved.

▷ **Answer the questions about page 351 of** *Parrots Over Puerto Rico.*

1. What problem do the parrots face and how do they solve it?

    _____

    _____

2. What problem do the Boricuas face? What is their solution?

    _____

    _____

    _____

▷ **Answer the question about page 355.**

3. How does the Puerto Rican Parrot Recovery Program plan to solve the problem of the declining parrot population?

    _____

    _____

▷ **Answer the question about page 360.**

4. What problems do scientists at the Río Abajo Aviary have to solve?

    _____

    _____

    _____

    _____

Name _____

Latin Root *bene*; Prefix *mal*–; Suffix –ure

> Complete the chart by predicting the meaning of each word using your knowledge of the root, prefix, and suffix to help you. Then use a print or online dictionary to confirm your predictions.

Word	I think it means...	Dictionary definition
benediction		
benefactor		
maltreat		
composure		
moisture		

> Write a sentence for each word in the chart.

_____

_____

_____

_____

_____

_____

_____

Text and Graphic Features

Text and graphic features are visual pieces of information included in a text. An author uses text and graphic features to help explain information.

▶ **Answer the questions about the illustrations on pages 346–347 of** *Parrots Over Puerto Rico.*

1. What places do the illustrations help you visualize?

_____

_____

_____

2. How do the illustrations and the text work together to introduce the story of the Puerto Rican parrots?

_____

_____

_____

_____

▶ **Answer the questions about the illustration on page 361.**

3. How does the illustration help you better understand the text?

_____

_____

_____

4. Which details in the illustration make the danger more vivid?

_____

_____

_____

Recognize Root Words with Spelling Changes

> Read each sentence. Underline the word in the sentence whose root has a spelling change. Then write the root word on the blank below.

1. Ayana edited the novel and translated it from English to French.

   root word: _____

2. The head chef dictated what would appear on the menu.

   root word: _____

3. Michelle likes participating in a touring theater company.

   root word: _____

4. I regret consuming that bowl of ice cream before going to bed.

   root word: _____

5. Charlie got involved in the computer club as a way of supporting his friend.

   root word: _____

6. The pet sitters demanded to be paid for providing cat food.

   root word: _____

7. Khalil collected more than 300 books and donated them to a local library.

   root word: _____

8. Abe wished he had not meddled in his friend's business.

   root word: _____

Name _____

Text Structure

Cause and effect is a type of **text structure** an author uses to organize ideas in a text. An author uses the cause-and-effect structure to explain what happened and why it happened.

▶ **Answer the questions about text structure on page 353 of** *Parrots Over Puerto Rico.*

1. What causes the parrots to begin to disappear?

_____

_____

_____

2. Do you think this change has a big impact on the parrots? Cite evidence from the text to support your response.

_____

_____

_____

_____

_____

_____

3. In paragraph 20, what other human actions were causing the parrots to disappear?

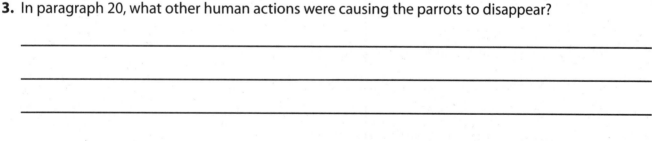

_____

_____

_____

Name _____

Recognize Root Words with Spelling Changes

▷ **Read the first sentence in each pair. Look at the underlined word and identify its root word. Write that root word in the blank in the second sentence of the pair.**

1. I hope tomorrow will be <u>sunnier</u>.

Today is not very _____ .

2. There are several <u>ferries</u> that carry people across the river.

The captain of the _____ had crossed the river many times.

3. We were cold after ice-skating, but Mom's hot chocolate made us feel <u>cozier</u>.

The fire in the fireplace also made us feel _____ .

4. Alaska is the <u>iciest</u> state of all!

However, Minnesota is also very _____ in the winter.

5. The general was famous for his brilliant <u>strategies</u>.

He developed a new _____ to win the battle.

6. Ben thinks it's fun to be <u>terrified</u>.

He goes to scary movies that _____ his friends.

7. Harper would like to win many <u>trophies</u> for martial arts.

She just won her first _____ last week.

8. I have many happy <u>memories</u> of my grandmother.

My earliest _____ is of us baking together.

Name _____

Critical Vocabulary

You can use the words you learn from reading as you talk and write.

> **Use details from *Christo and Jeanne-Claude* to support your answers to the questions below. Then use the Critical Vocabulary words as you talk with a partner about your answers.**

1. Why was there **controversy** about constructing The Gates?

_____

2. Why were some people **skeptical** about the project?

_____

3. What actions show Christo and Jeanne-Claude's **persistence**?

_____

4. What made The Gates an **ambitious** project?

_____

5. Explain this statement: "The Gates were **gracing** the paths of Central Park."

_____

6. What are some of the tasks that were **incorporated** into the work of building The Gates?

_____

7. What was **ingenious** about The Gates?

_____

Name _____

8. What had to be **manufactured** in order to create The Gates?

_____

9. Why did the gates that **traversed** the paths vary in width?

_____

▶ **Write a sentence that uses one of the vocabulary words.**

_____

_____

_____

Name _____

Central Idea

The **central idea** is what a text is mostly about. Relevant details tell more about the central idea and help readers understand it. Relevant details may include facts, examples, or definitions. In order to determine the central idea of a text, readers need to look at the details carefully. Then they need to ask themselves what one idea the details tell about.

> **Answer these questions about the central idea on page 20, paragraph 3, of** *Christo and Jeanne-Claude.*

1. What is the central idea?

_____

_____

2. What is one relevant idea that supports the central idea?

_____

_____

_____

3. Why is it important to identify and understand this central idea?

_____

_____

_____

> **Answer this additional question about the central idea on page 22.**

4. What is the central idea of paragraphs 9–12?

_____

_____

Name _____

Recognize Root Words with Spelling Changes

▶ **Read the paragraph. For each blank, choose the word from the box that works best in the sentence. Use a word only once.**

duties	duty	earlier	early
horrified	horrify	denied	deny
abilities	ability	greediest	greedy
scariest	scary	enemies	enemy

The gamers were about to begin a new role-playing game. A day _____ ,

they had rolled the dice to find out what _____ and skills their characters

would have. Jamie, the party leader, assigned people different _____ to

carry out on the quest. Destiny, whose character was the biggest and strongest, was

_____ to be told that she would have all the dirty jobs. Tomás wanted his

character to be a _____ elf who was always stealing from the others. But

he _____ it when the others pointed that out. Ivan wanted to find the

group's many _____ , so the group would be prepared for danger. Lori just

wanted to be sure their mission would have lots of frightening moments. "Make it

the _____ game we've ever played!" she told Ivan's mom, who helped set up

the game for them.

Name _____

Latin Root **struct**; Prefix **de**; Suffixes **-ion**, **-ism**

The word **construct** contains a root that has Latin origins. The meaning of the root **struct** is "build." The prefix **de-** (removing something, the opposite of) and the suffixes **-ion** and **-ism** (an action, process, state, or condition) are found in words such as **deconstruct**, **deconstruction**, and **constructionism**.

▶ **Complete the chart with other words that contain the root** **struct**, **prefix** **de-**, **and the suffixes** **-ion** **and** **-ism**.

struct	de–
_____	_____
_____	_____
_____	_____
–ion	**–ism**
_____	_____
_____	_____
_____	_____

▶ **Choose one word from each category and use it in a sentence.**

_____

_____

_____

_____

_____

Name _____

Text Structure

Sequence is a type of text structure. Authors use sequence structure to tell the order in which things or events follow each other. Authors might use this structure to share steps for solving a problem, or to discuss steps in a process.

▶ **Answer the questions about text structure in *Christo and Jeanne-Claude* on page 21.**

1. What procedure do the authors explain in paragraphs 7–8?

_____

_____

2. What were the steps that the 600 workers took?

_____

_____

_____

_____

3. What is the authors' purpose in using a sequence text structure?

_____

_____

_____

▶ **Answer the question about text structure in *Christo and Jeanne-Claude* on page 28.**

4. What text structure do the authors use on this page? How do you know?

_____

_____

_____

Author's Craft

The **tone** of a text is the author's attitude toward its subject or characters. An author's tone can be conveyed through the use of voice, style, and word choice.

▶ **Answer the questions about author's tone in paragraph 20 on page 25 of *Christo and Jeanne-Claude.***

1. What words would you use to describe the tone of the writing?

_____

_____

2. How does the authors' choice of words convey tone?

_____

_____

_____

_____

Suffixes: –ful, –ly, –ness, –less, –ment

▶ **Read each sentence. Find the words that have the suffixes** *–ful*, *–ly*, *–ness*, *–less*, **and** *–ment*. **Underline these suffixes.**

1. It was an eventful afternoon with school, the baseball game, and a birthday party.

2. She gets a lot of fulfillment from her job as a teacher.

3. The fans' level of excitement at the soccer game was high.

4. I try hard to be thoughtful in all of my schoolwork.

5. In his eagerness to get to the door, Sanjay tripped over a big bag of blocks.

6. The scribbles seemed meaningless to everyone.

7. Laura sent a get-well card to her sister, who is recovering from an illness.

8. You need to move quickly, or we will be late.

9. He ate the snack so hungrily that I wondered if he had eaten anything else all day.

10. Try not to be careless when wiping up the milk you spilled.

Name _____

Critical Vocabulary

You can use the words you learn from reading as you talk and write.

▶ **Use details from *Rita Moreno* to support your answers to the questions below. Then use the Critical Vocabulary words as you talk with a partner about your answers.**

1. Although Rita was getting public **exposure**, why was it difficult for her to get the types of acting roles she was looking for in her early career?

   _____

2. What did Rita Moreno do in order to find new roles and not just **stereotypical** roles?

   _____

3. How did earning the Presidential Medal of Freedom help end many **discriminatory** practices in Hollywood?

   _____

   _____

4. Why did the fact that Rita was **authentic** increase her popularity?

   _____

5. What did Rita's role as the **willful** Anita have in common with Rita herself?

   _____

▶ **Choose two of the Critical Vocabulary words and use them in sentences.**

   _____

   _____

   _____

   _____

Characters

Good biography writers work hard to help readers get to know the person in the text. They bring a **subject** or **character** to life by sharing details about his or her appearance, traits, actions, choices, and feelings. Doing so allows readers to understand the person's life and share in his or her experiences.

▶ **Answer the question about characters on page 36 of *Rita Moreno*.**

1. What can you infer from the final quotation in paragraph 8?

_____

_____

_____

_____

▶ **Answer this additional question about *Rita Moreno*.**

2. How would you describe the character of Rita Moreno? How did her behavior help you understand what she was like?

_____

_____

_____

_____

_____

Suffixes: –ful, –ly, –ness, –less, –ment

▶ In each sentence, there is a word that needs a suffix. Choose a suffix from the box that will complete the word and make sense in the sentence.

–ful	–ly	–ness	–less	–ment

1. The two groups signed an agree_____ to complete the work on the building.

2. The couple celebrated their engage_____ to be married with their families and friends.

3. She walked dangerous_____ close to the edge of the cliff.

4. The cat sat completely motion_____ as it waited for the mouse to get close.

5. This tool is so power_____ that it will finish the job in minutes.

6. I am grate_____ that you came to celebrate with us.

7. Be aware of the healthi_____ of foods, so that you eat a balanced diet.

8. It seemed as though the light magical_____ appeared as soon as she said the word *on*.

9. I was too weak to open the heavy door, which made me feel power_____ .

10. She needed to rely on her clever_____ to be able to solve the problem.

Critical Vocabulary

You can use the words you learn from reading as you talk and write.

▶ **Read each sentence. Circle the sentence that best fits the meaning of the word in dark print.**

1. bars

Please play a few happy songs.

Please play a small part of the song.

2. contagious

Soon after the band started playing, everyone was singing along.

Soon after the band started playing, everyone had left the hall.

3. fever

The crowd was disappointed in the new band.

The crowd was excited to hear the new band.

4. duets

The violinist played after the pianist had finished.

The pianist and violinist played together beautifully.

5. solos

The two singers' voices made great harmony.

The singer's voice soared throughout the hall.

▶ **Choose two of the Critical Vocabulary words and use them in a sentence.**

_____

_____

_____

Name _____

Point of View

Point of view refers to who tells a story, or the narrator of that story. A first-person narrator is part of the story and uses the pronouns *I* or *me*. A third-person narrator is a supporting character or someone outside of the story who uses pronouns like *he* or *she*.

> **Answer the questions about point of view on page 48, paragraph 21 of *Play, Louis, Play!***

1. Who is telling the story of Louis Armstrong?

_____

_____

2. From what point of view is the story told? How do you know?

_____

_____

3. What is the effect of writing in the first-person point of view?

_____

_____

_____

_____

> **Answer this additional question about point of view.**

4. What is the effect of writing in the third-person point of view? How is it different from first-person point of view?

_____

_____

_____

_____

Name _____

Prefixes super- and micro-

The prefix *super–* has a Latin origin and means "more", "bigger", "better", or "beyond". The prefix *micro–* comes from the Greek word *micros*, meaning "tiny".

▶ **Complete the chart with other words that contain the prefixes *super–* and *micro–*.**

super–	*micro–*
_____	_____
_____	_____
_____	_____
_____	_____

▶ **Choose one word from each category and use it in a sentence.**

_____

_____

_____

_____

Name _____

Author's Craft

An **author's craft** is made up of all the techniques the author uses to make his or her writing strong. It is how he or she communicates ideas to the reader. Part of an author's craft is the author's voice, or individual writing style.

> Answer the questions about author's craft on page 49 of *Play, Louis, Play!*

1. How would you describe the narrator's voice?

_____

_____

_____

2. What does the author's use of the word "c-c-cold" make you think about the narrator?

_____

_____

_____

> Answer this additional question about the author's craft.

3. How is the reader affected by this type of voice for the narrator?

_____

_____

_____

_____

_____

_____

Name _____

Words from Other Languages

> Read each sentence and look at the underlined word. Use a print or online dictionary to look up the word. Circle the answer that shows how the underlined word is pronounced.

1. Guitar is a Spanish word. I like to hear guitar music.

   gih-TAHR   jih-TAHR

2. Buoy is a word that has Dutch origins. A buoy floats on the surface of a body of water.

   BOO-ee   BUH-oy

3. Hibachi is a Japanese word. A hibachi is a small, portable grill.

   HIH-bach-eye   hih-BAH-chee

4. Dolphin is a word that has Greek origins. Dolphins are intelligent animals.

   DAWLP-hin   DAWL-fin

5. Borscht is a word from Russia. Borscht is a soup made from beets.

   borsht   borskt

6. Quiche is a French word. Quiche is an egg-based pie.

   KWICH-ee   keesh

7. Canyon is a Spanish word. Canyons are often formed by rivers.

   KAN-yun   KAN-ee-awn

8. Canoe is a Spanish word. You'll need a paddle or an oar to steer a canoe.

   KAN-oh-ee   kuh-NOO

Name _____

Critical Vocabulary

You can use the words you learn from reading as you talk and write.

> **Use what you learned about the vocabulary words from *Phillis's Big Test* to help you finish each sentence.**

_____

1. The man was **testifying** about _____.

2. The **outcome** of my math test was _____.

3. My grandmother is proud of her **homeland** because _____.

4. I **consented** to _____ because _____

_____.

5. The woman carried a **sheaf** of _____ in order to _____

_____.

6. My parents **advised** me to _____.

7. After the game, he was **content** to _____.

> **Choose two of the Critical Vocabulary words and use them in a sentence.**

_____

_____

_____

_____

Name _____

Theme

The **theme** of a text is the most important message or life lesson the author wants readers to understand. The main character's or subject's thoughts and actions can give readers clues to a text's theme.

> **Answer the questions about paragraphs 9 and 10 on page 58 of *Phillis's Big Test*.**

1. What are these paragraphs mainly about?

_____

_____

2. What do these paragraphs tell you about what Phillis thinks is important?

_____

_____

3. What theme is the author introducing here?

_____

_____

> **Answer the questions about paragraphs 11 and 12 on page 60 of *Phillis's Big Test*.**

4. What do you know about the attitudes of the Wheatley family?

_____

_____

5. Why might this be unusual under the circumstances?

_____

_____

_____

_____

Name _____

Suffixes –ant/–ent; Latin Roots port, duc/duct

The suffixes *–ant* and *–ent* often appear in nouns and adjectives of Latin origin, such as *pursuant*, *accountant*, and *adolescent*. The words *transported* and *production* both contain a Latin root. The meaning of the root *port* is "carry." The meaning of the root *duct* or *duc* is "lead."

> **Complete the chart with other words that contain the roots *port* and *duc/duct* and the suffixes *–ant* and *–ent*.**

–ant	–ent
_____	_____
_____	_____
_____	_____

port	duc/duct
_____	_____
_____	_____
_____	_____

> **Choose one word from each category and use it in a sentence.**

_____

_____

_____

_____

Literary Elements

Authors use **literary elements** such as historical and cultural **setting** to provide context for a story or a set of true events. Analyzing a text's setting can help readers understand its subject or main character and what happens in his or her life.

> **Answer the questions about the setting on page 57 of** *Phillis's Big Test*.

1. In what time period is this biography set?

_____

_____

2. What details does the illustration show about the biography's setting?

_____

_____

_____

_____

> **Now answer this additional question about the setting.**

3. The author says that Phillis learned to appreciate "her very own role in the chain of events stretching from past to present." What does she mean?

_____

_____

_____

_____

Name _____

Words from Other Languages

> **Read each sentence and look at the underlined word. Use a print or online dictionary to look up the word. Circle the answer that shows how the underlined word is pronounced.**

1. Iguana is a Spanish word. An iguana is a large lizard.

        IG-oo-a-nuh   ih-GWAH-nuh

2. Denim is a French word. My blue jeans are made of denim cloth.

        DEN-im   DEE-nim

3. Umbrella is an Italian word. My umbrella turned inside-out in the windstorm.

        um-BREL-uh   UM-brel-uh

4. Jungle is a word from Hindi. Jungles are often very hot and humid.

        JUN-gul   JUN-gluh

5. Coleslaw is a Dutch word. Coleslaw usually has cabbage in it.

        KOH-luh-slaw   KOHL-slaw

6. Spaghetti is an Italian word. Spaghetti with tomato sauce is my favorite!

        spug-HEH-tee   spuh-GEH-tee

7. Receipt is a French word. A receipt is proof that you paid for something.

        rih-SEET   RUH-keept

8. Ketchup is a word from Chinese. My sister puts ketchup on her eggs!

        KET-chup   KECH-up

Name _____

Figurative Language

Authors create vivid descriptions by using **figurative language**, or words and phrases that go beyond their literal meaning. Common types of figurative language include similes, metaphors, hyperbole, and personification. Analyzing the author's use of figurative language can provide a better understanding of important themes and ideas in a text.

> **Answer the questions about paragraph 16 on page 61 of *Phillis's Big Test*.**

1. What kind of figurative language is "danced in her head"?

_____

_____

2. What does this use of figurative language help you understand about Phillis?

_____

_____

_____

_____

Name _____

Final Stable Syllables –ain, –ture, –sure

▶ Each sentence has an underlined word with the final syllable *–ain, –ture,* or *–sure*. Beneath each sentence, underline the correct pronunciation of the final syllable in the underlined word.

1. We are excited for our adventure to the rock-climbing park.

/chər/ /zhər/

2. Use the ruler to measure how long the table is.

/chər/ /zhər/

3. Antonio was thirsty, so he took a drink from the water fountain.

/ən/ /ān/

4. Rachel always arrives on time, so I am certain she won't be late today.

/ĕn/ /n/

5. Joe's back injury made it torture to lift anything heavy.

/chər/ /zhər/

6. It's too bright in here, so please close the curtain.

/n/ /ān/

7. It was a pleasure to visit with our whole family.

/chər/ /zhər/

8. The light bulb is burned out in that light fixture.

/chər/ /zhər/

Name _____

Critical Vocabulary

You can use the words you learn from reading as you talk and write.

> **Use details from _Into the Unknown_ to support your answers to the questions below. Use the word line to answer each question. Then explain your answer. Use the Critical Vocabulary words as you talk with a partner about your answers.**

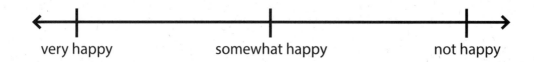

very happy   somewhat happy   not happy

How happy would you be if . . .

1. you began to **ascend** from the ground?

_____

2. you had to race across a **vast** field?

_____

3. your car door was **forged** shut?

_____

4. your teacher introduced a new **principle** in science class?

_____

5. a **cosmic** visitor came to your class?

_____

6. mariners asked you to work with them for one year?

_____

> **Choose two of the Critical Vocabulary words and use them in a sentence.**

_____

_____

_____

Name _____

Text Structure

Authors of informational texts often use a cause-and-effect **text structure** to explain what happened and why it happened. One way to recognize cause-and-effect text structure is through the author's use of transition words or phrases such as *because*, *so*, *in order to*, and *as a result*.

▶ **Answer the questions about paragraphs 5–6 on page 83 of** *Into the Unknown: Above and Below.*

1. How does the author organize, or structure, ideas in this part of the text?

_____

_____

_____

2. What words or phrases help you understand each step of the balloon's movement?

_____

_____

3. Why does the author use this structure?

_____

_____

▶ **Answer the questions about page 86.**

4. How does the author organize, or structure, this part of the text? How do you know?

_____

_____

5. What words or phrases help you understand the chronology, or order, of events?

_____

_____

Name _____

Final Stable Syllables -ain, -ture, -sure

> Read each sentence. Choose the word with the final stable syllable –ain, –ture, or –sure from the box below that best completes each sentence.

–ain words	bargain, certain, mountain
–ture words	moisture, miniature, furniture
–sure words	enclosure, displeasure

1. The teacher expressed her _____ by scolding the students.

2. Kim skied down the steep _____ .

3. Shaila collected _____ dolls for her dollhouse.

4. At a cost of two for $1, these snacks are a _____ .

5. The painters moved the _____ when they painted the room.

6. Are you _____ that's the shirt you want to buy?

7. The _____ in the air made my hair get frizzy!

8. It started to rain, so we moved the party into the _____ .

Latin Roots *tract, chron, gress*

The words *extract*, *chronology*, and *progress* contain Latin roots. The meaning of the root *tract* is "to pull." The meaning of the root *chron* is "time," and the meaning of the root *gress* is "to move or step."

▶ Complete the chart with other words that contain the roots *tract*, *chron*, and *gress*.

tract	chron
_____	_____
_____	_____
_____	_____

gress
_____
_____
_____

▶ Choose one word from each category and use it in a sentence.

_____

_____

_____

_____

_____

_____

Name _____

Text and Graphic Features

Authors of informational texts often include **text features** (such as introductions, **bold words**, **headings**, and **glossaries**) and **graphic features** (such as diagrams, **illustrations**, **graphs**, **charts**, maps, and timelines) to help explain or elaborate on the information in the text.

> **Answer the questions about the diagram on page 82 of** *Into the Unknown: Above and Below.*

1. What does the diagram explain?

_____

_____

2. What key idea in paragraphs 1–2 does the diagram support?

_____

_____

_____

> **Answer these additional questions from pages 83–85.**

3. How does the diagram on pages 84–85 help you understand the text on page 83?

_____

_____

_____

4. How does the diagram add to your understanding of the Piccards' balloon project?

_____

_____

_____

Name _____

Content-Area Words

Authors of informational texts often use **content-area words**, or words that are specific to a particular area of study. Examples are areas such as math, social studies, science, sports, music, and art. Authors might put these words in boldface to make them stand out. Sometimes content-area words are different uses of **multiple-meaning words**. Readers can often use **context** clues to figure out the meaning of unfamiliar content-area words.

▶ **Answer the questions about pages 84–85 of** *Into the Unknown: Above and Below.*

1. The word *hatch* has more than one meaning. Which meaning is being used in this text?

_____

_____

2. What helps you understand this meaning of *hatch*?

_____

_____

_____

▶ **Answer this additional question about the author's use of content-area words in** *Into the Unknown: Above and Below.*

3. The author uses a number of content-area words that apply to the parts and fittings of the gondola. How does the use of these words help your understanding of the text?

_____

_____

_____

_____

_____

Name _____

Unstressed Final Syllables

> **Read each sentence. Find the word that has the unstressed final syllable /ĭj/ (as in** *image*), **/ĭv/(as in** *olive*), **or /ĭs/ (as in** *office*) **and underline it.**

1. Joey reluctantly took out the garbage during the rainstorm.

2. The wrongly accused man received justice in court.

3. The hotel employee carried my luggage to my room.

4. The colorful rattle was attractive to the young baby.

5. The food and service at the new restaurant is excellent.

6. Carla read the literature passage fluently and with dramatic expression!

7. The creative student wanted to become a novelist.

8. The tallest kid had an advantage on the basketball court.

Name _____

Critical Vocabulary

You can use the words you learn from reading as you talk and write.

> **Use details and ideas from *Great Discoveries* to support your answers to the questions below. Then use the Critical Vocabulary words as you talk with a partner about your answers.**

1. How was the land on the **outskirts** of Machu Picchu used?

_____

2. Who **ransacked** many Inca cities?

_____

3. What is something that a **ruthless** emperor might do?

_____

4. Who are some of the top **authorities** in a country?

_____

_____

5. Why is the artwork in the Lascaux caves so **precious**?

_____

_____

> **Choose two of the Critical Vocabulary words and use them in a sentence.**

_____

_____

_____

_____

Name _____

Central Idea

The **central idea** is what a text is mostly about. Relevant **details** tell more about the central idea and help readers understand it. Relevant details may include facts, examples, or definitions. In order to determine the central idea of a text, readers need to look at the relevant details carefully. Then they need to ask themselves, "What is the one idea all the relevant details tell about?"

▶ **Answer these questions about the central idea on page 101 of** *Great Discoveries and Amazing Adventures.*

1. What is the central idea of the "Ancient Pictures in a Hidden Cave" section? Cite in your response relevant details that support the text.

_____

_____

_____

2. What message about archaeological discoveries is the author sharing?

_____

_____

_____

▶ **Answer these additional questions about the central idea.**

3. What is the overall central idea of the selection?

_____

_____

_____

4. What relevant details from the text support the central idea?

_____

_____

_____

Name _____

Unstressed Final Syllables

▶ **Read each sentence. Find the word that has the unstressed final syllable /ĭj/ (as in** *image*)**, /ĭv/(as in** *creative*)**, or /ĭs/ (as in** *office*)**) and underline it.**

1. The salad had carrots, broccoli, cabbage, and lettuce.

2. The small cottage had no garage.

3. I heard the message when I was backstage at the play.

4. Kevin saw that spices had collected in a tiny crevice.

5. What motive could someone have to steal a birdcage?

6. A doctor put a bandage on the teenage boy's ankle.

7. He felt outrage at being held hostage.

8. I will demonstrate correct usage of the device.

Critical Vocabulary

You can use the words you learn from reading as you talk and write.

▶ **Use what you know about the vocabulary words from _Space Ship One_ to help you complete the following activity. Read each sentence. Circle the sentence which best fits the meaning of the word in dark print. Then use the Critical Vocabulary words as you talk with a partner about your answers.**

1. ignited

I was shocked by how quickly the sparks started the fire.
The firefighters came just in time to extinguish the flames.

2. hybrid

The rose is one of the oldest types of known flowers.
The scientist made a new flower from a rose and an iris.

3. synthetic

Most of my clothes are not made from natural fabrics.
All of my shirts are made from pure cotton.

4. exhaust

I enjoy the clean air at the lake.
The pollution in this town is high because there are so many cars.

5. physics

I really enjoyed dissecting a frog in science lab today.
I built an experiment using levers and pulleys.

6. institution

I am thinking about starting a new business.
My mother works for a charitable organization that offers resources to those who need it.

▶ **Choose two of the Critical Vocabulary words and use them in a sentence.**

_____

_____

Name _____

Author's Craft

Author's craft is the way that an author makes his or her writing interesting. It is how he or she communicates ideas to the reader. Part of author's craft is the author's **voice**. This refers to his or her individual writing style. It is what makes the writing unique. An author's voice can be funny or serious, formal or informal. Word choice helps to create an author's voice.

▷ **Answer these questions about author's craft on page 114 of** *SpaceShipOne*.

1. Which words and phrases show how Matthew felt as the spaceship came back to Earth?

_____

_____

_____

_____

2. How does this first-person account contribute to the text?

_____

_____

_____

_____

Name _____

Prefixes mega-, sub-; Latin Roots ped, dent

The word *megadose* contains the prefix *mega-* which means "large." The word *submerge* contains the prefix *sub-* which means "under."

The word *pedestrian* contains a root that has Latin origins. The meaning of the root *ped* is "foot." The word *dentist* also contains a root that has Latin origins. The meaning of the root *dent* is "tooth."

> **Complete the chart with other words that contain the prefixes *mega-* and *sub-* and the roots *ped* and *dent*.**

mega-	sub-
ped	dent

> **Choose a word from each category and use it in a sentence.**

_____

_____

_____

_____

Name _____

Author's Purpose

The **author's purpose** is the author's reason for writing a story or text. Authors usually write to persuade, to inform, to entertain, or to teach a lesson. Knowing a writer's purpose helps readers recognize the author's message.

> **Answer these questions about author's purpose on pages 115–116 of *SpaceShipOne*.**

1. What is the author's purpose in writing this text? How do you know?

_____

_____

_____

2. How do the photos with captions help inform the reader?

_____

_____

_____

Name _____

Unstressed Syllables

▸ **Write the word from the box that best completes each sentence. Make sure the word has the unstressed syllable that is noted in the section heading.**

syrup	sugar	surprise	liter
western	pursuit	perform	trouble

First Syllable Unstressed

1. Becca planned a _____ party for her sister.

2. Kasia will _____ a new dance routine.

3. The police are in _____ of the thief.

Second Syllable Unstressed

4. Farhan poured _____ on his pancakes.

5. The sun sank slowly in the _____ sky.

6. Skyler took a _____ of water on the hike.

7. Al did not want to get in _____, so he followed the rules.

8. The first step is to mix the _____ and butter.

Critical Vocabulary

You can use the words you learn from reading as you talk and write.

> Use what you learned about the vocabulary words from *Mighty Mars Rovers* to help you finish each sentence. Then use the Critical Vocabulary words as you talk with a partner about your answers.

1. The little girl **resembled** her . . .

_____

2. As we looked out at the **expanse** of land, we knew . . .

_____

3. Once my email is **transmitted** . . .

_____

4. I took my **ailing** computer to . . .

_____

5. To finish the project on time we need to **deploy** . . .

_____

6. The **transition** from summer to fall usually . . .

_____

7. Traveling over this **terrain** will mean . . .

_____

8. **International** travel can be . . .

_____

> Choose two of the Critical Vocabulary words and use them in a sentence.

_____

_____

Name _____

Central Idea

The **central idea** is the most important thought of a story or text that is supported by relevant details. Sometimes an author clearly states the central idea. Sometimes it's implied, or suggested, and the reader has to figure it out using evidence in the text.

▶ **Answer the questions about the central idea on pages 122–123 of** *The Mighty Mars Rovers.*

1. What is the central idea of pages 122–123?

_____

_____

2. What relevant details support this central idea?

_____

_____

_____

_____

▶ **Answer these questions about the central idea on pages 124–125.**

3. What is the central idea of pages 124–125?

_____

_____

_____

_____

4. What relevant details support this central idea?

_____

_____

_____

Name _____

Latin Root terr; Prefixes aqua-, pro-, anti-

> Complete the chart by predicting the meaning of each word using your knowledge of the root and prefixes. Then use a print or online dictionary to confirm your predictions.

Word	I think it means . . .	Dictionary Definitions
terrestrial		pertaining to the Earth
terrier		a small breed of dog used by hunters to dig in the ground for small game
aquaplane		a board pulled by a boat on the water that a person rides on
aquatic		taking place on the water
probiotic		a supplement to replace helpful bacteria in the body
antibiotic		a medicine to rid the body of harmful bacteria
provoke		to stir up or give rise to something; to cause
antidote		a medicine to counter the effects of poison

> Choose one word from each category and use it in a sentence.

_____

_____

_____

_____

_____

_____

_____

_____

Name _____

Author's Craft

Authors choose specific words—including **sensory words**, **metaphors**, and content-area words—to clearly make a point, to make a text interesting, and to make events and explanations easy to follow. Analyzing an author's word choice can help a reader visualize the details of a narrative and better understand the text.

▶ **Answer the questions about paragraph 37 on page 129 of** *The Mighty Mars Rovers.*

1. What imagery helps readers visualize how Opportunity's landing looks and sounds?

_____

_____

2. How do these word choices contribute meaning to the text?

_____

_____

▶ **Answer these additional questions about author's craft on page 132.**

3. In paragraph 49, what simile does the author use to describe how the Martian pebbles look? Why does the author describe the pebbles this way?

_____

_____

_____

4. What comparison does the author make in paragraph 51? What does this help readers understand?

_____

_____

_____

Name _____

Unstressed Syllables

▶ **Read each sentence. Then underline the number that shows how many unstressed syllables are in the underlined word.**

1. Sadie prefers <u>vanilla</u> yogurt.

          1   2

2. Imani and her brother rearranged the <u>furniture</u> in the room.

          2   3

3. Members of both political parties attended the <u>ceremony</u>.

          2   3

4. Kyle told his <u>employer</u> that he would be absent on Monday.

          1   2

5. The mad scientist had an evil plan to <u>dominate</u> the world.

          2   3

6. The concert was part of the town's annual <u>festival</u>.

          1   2

7. Marc used a <u>calculator</u> to help solve the math problem.

          3   4

8. The komodo dragon is a large and dangerous <u>monitor</u> lizard.

          1   2

Name _____

Text Structure

Text structure is the way an author organizes ideas and details in a text. Most narratives, or stories, are generally arranged in chronological text structure. Within a narrative text, however, an author might use cause-and-effect text structure to explain what happens and why it happens.

> **Answer the questions about paragraph 30 on page 126 of *The Mighty Mars Rovers*.**

1. What cause-and-effect relationships does the author explain in paragraph 30?

_____

_____

2. What is the author's purpose for including all of the "maybe" statements in the paragraph?

_____

_____

> **Answer another question about the cause-and-effect text structure in *The Mighty Mars Rovers*.**

3. What does the author's use of cause-and-effect text structure in this narrative help you understand about the work NASA scientists do?

_____

_____

_____

_____

Name _____

Homophones

> Choose the correct homophone within the parentheses to complete each sentence. Write the word on the blank.

1. The fox chased the (hair, hare) _____ through the woods.

2. Do not try to swim against the strong (current, currant) _____ .

3. He took off his hat, revealing his (bald, bawled) _____ head.

4. Keisha read her essay (allowed, aloud) _____ .

5. The full (weight, wait) _____ of the box made him stagger.

6. All the presents are finally (wrapped, rapped) _____ .

7. We watched a car drive (past, passed) _____ our house.

8. A dove is a (cymbal, symbol) _____ of peace.

9. He acts shy in the (presence, presents) _____ of strangers.

10. My mother stores jars of jam in the (seller, cellar) _____ .

Name _____

Critical Vocabulary

You can use the words you learn from reading as you talk and write.

▶ **Use what you learned about the vocabulary words from *A Movie in My Pillow* to help you finish each sentence. Then use the Critical Vocabulary words as you talk with a partner about your sentences.**

1. The children were **yearning** for . . .

_____

2. A **civil** war broke out between . . .

_____

3. I decided to **dedicate** . . .

_____

4. The business was **flourishing** because . . .

_____

5. I am **fortunate** to have . . .

_____

6. **Discarded** objects are sometimes useful because . . .

_____

7. One way that I am similar to my **relatives** is . . .

_____

▶ **Use two of the Critical Vocabulary words in a single sentence.**

_____

_____

_____

Name _____

Theme

The **theme** of a poem is the lesson a poet wants readers to learn. Theme might also be called a moral, or lesson. Sometimes the theme is stated in the text. Other times, the theme is implied, and readers have to look for clues and make inferences about the theme. Identifying the theme in a poem can help readers determine the **author's purpose** for writing.

> **Answer these questions about theme in *A Movie in My Pillow*.**

1. How does the speaker feel about leaving El Salvador?

_____

_____

_____

_____

2. What challenges does he face in his new home? How does he respond?

_____

_____

_____

_____

3. What message, or theme, does the author want to share?

_____

_____

_____

_____

Name _____

Homophones

▶ Choose the correct word from the box to complete each sentence. Write the word on the blank.

ceiling	whether	band	medal	throne
sealing	weather	banned	meddle	thrown

1. Eliza plays flute in the middle school _____.

2. I wish you would stop trying to _____ in my life.

3. At the museum, we saw a _____ of an ancient king.

4. Andre could not decide _____ to go swimming.

5. After _____ the envelope, Janine put a stamp on it.

6. The _____ report calls for a foot of snow tomorrow.

7. Smoking is _____ on all trains and buses.

8. Rafael got a _____ for winning the chess tournament.

9. Last week, a baseball was _____ through that window by accident.

10. There is a spider crawling across the _____!

Name _____

Prefixes uni–, mono–, bi–, tri–, multi–

The prefixes *uni–* and *mono–* mean "one" and are found in words such as *united* and *monologue*. The prefixes *bi–* and *tri–* mean "two" and "three" and are found in words such as *bilingual* and *trilingual*. The prefix *multi–* means "many" and is found in words such as *multilingual*.

> **Complete the chart with other words that contain the prefixes *uni–*, *mono–*, *bi–*, *tri–*, and *multi–*.**

uni–	mono–	multi–
_____	_____	_____
_____	_____	_____
_____	_____	_____
bi–	**tri–**	
_____	_____	
_____	_____	
_____	_____	

> **Choose one word from each category and use it in a sentence.**

_____

_____

_____

_____

_____

_____

_____

Elements of Poetry

When authors write poems, they use **elements of poetry** to communicate their ideas, create a mood, or make readers look at something in a fresh way. Many use **figurative language** to compare one thing to something else. Similes, metaphors, and personification are examples of figurative language. Poets also use sound devices. For example, **repetition**—the repeating of a word or phrase over and over—draws attention to a specific idea and adds to the mood and rhythm of a poem.

> **Answer these questions about elements of poetry from page 155 of *A Movie in My Pillow*.**

1. What happens in the first stanza?

_____

_____

2. How does the author use elements of poetry to reveal the speaker's feelings about this experience?

_____

_____

3. What clues about the theme do the speaker's reflections provide?

_____

_____

> **Answer these questions about elements of poetry from page 169.**

4. How does the speaker describe the flowers?

_____

5. What feature do the mountains have?

_____

6. What do the buildings do?

_____

Author's Craft

The **tone** of a poem reflects the way the author or the speaker feels about the subject of the poem. An author chooses words carefully to create a tone that suits his or her purpose for writing. Recognizing the tone and knowing how the author feels about the subject helps readers understand the author's ideas and message more clearly.

> **Answer these questions about tone on page 161 of _A Movie in My Pillow_.**

1. What words and phrases does the speaker use to describe Papa's truck?

_____

_____

2. What overall tone does the speaker create in this poem?

_____

_____

> **Answer this additional question about tone.**

3. How does the speaker's tone affect your reading of a poem?

_____

_____

s_____

_____

Name _____

Prefixes: in-, un-, dis-, mis-

> ▶ Read each sentence. Find the words that have the prefixes *in–*, *un–*, *dis–*, and *mis–*. Underline these prefixes.

1. Luisa wore an informal outfit to the barbeque.

2. Jessica mislaid her keys and couldn't find them.

3. The disorder in this drawer makes it hard to find my socks.

4. To enjoy the hike to the top of the cliff, you must be unafraid of heights.

5. I don't think Joe meant to cut the cake into pieces of unequal sizes.

6. During class, Mia's attention was misdirected out the window.

7. My dog disobeyed my command to get off the couch.

8. It was inconsiderate that you did not tell me you would be late.

Name _____

Critical Vocabulary

You can use the words you learn from reading as you talk and write.

> **Use details and ideas using *From Scratch* to support your answers to the questions below. Then use the Critical Vocabulary words as you talk with a partner about your answers.**

1. Why could you say that Priya's mother **nudged** her to make friends?

_____

2. What are some examples of Priya's mother's **reserve**?

_____

3. What **casual** clothing does Priya's mother wear on the first day of school?

_____

4. What is something that Priya does **reluctantly**?

_____

> **Choose two of the Critical Vocabulary words and use them in a sentence.**

_____

_____

_____

_____

Name _____

Literary Elements

Authors of realistic fiction use **literary elements**—including **plot** and **conflict**—to develop a **story structure** that relates the events to the characters' experiences. Analyzing a story's plot and conflicts can help a reader understand what happens to the characters and why.

▶ **Answer the questions about the conflicts that characters face from pages 176–181 of** *From Scratch.*

1. What problem does Priya face?

_____

_____

_____

2. Which events give you clues about how Priya feels?

_____

_____

_____

_____

_____

_____

▶ **Answer the questions about conflict and resolution from pages 182–184.**

3. What is the first event that will likely lead to the problem's solution?

_____

_____

4. What is the second event that will likely lead to the solution?

_____

_____

Name _____

Prefixes: *in-, un-, dis-, mis-*

> In each sentence, there is a word that needs a prefix. Choose a prefix from the box that will complete the word and make sense in the sentence.

in-	un-	dis-	mis-

1. The expensive dress she wanted was entirely _____affordable.

2. Let's take our time to _____cover everything about this playground.

3. I got dressed in the dark and ended up wearing _____matched socks.

4. Ted lost points because his assignment was _____complete.

5. Juan was _____certain about the best way to complete the task.

6. Having started late, Lee was at a(n) _____advantage in the race.

7. The way you are speaking is rude and _____sensitive to others.

8. Be careful not to _____interpret the directions.

Critical Vocabulary

You can use the words you learn from reading as you talk and write.

▶ Use details from *Elisa's Diary* to support your answers to the activity below. Read each sentence. Circle the sentence that best fits the meaning of the word in dark print. Then use the Critical Vocabulary words as you talk with a partner about your answers.

1. diary

I wrote in my notebook about what I did today.
I wrote a composition for English class.

2. promptly

It took days for my friend to answer my email.
My friend answered my email right away.

3. semidarkness

We stumbled in the dim light.
We squinted in the brilliant sunshine.

4. obvious

The solution to the problem is hard to figure out.
The solution to the problem is easy to see.

5. comprehended

I was confused by what you said.
I understood you right away.

6. officially

Some people took the day off and went to the beach.
The governor declared today a state holiday.

Name _____

7. preliminary

The artist put the final touches on the painting.

The artist made sketches before starting to paint.

▶ **Choose two of the Critical Vocabulary words and use them in a sentence.**

_____

_____

Name _____

Characters

An author uses different literary elements—including **characters**—as the building blocks of a story. An author develops a character through the character's appearance, traits, behaviors, voice and dialogue, and thoughts and emotions, as well as through the way the character relates or compares to others in the story. Paying attention to what characters say, do, and learn helps readers discover the author's message, or theme.

▶ **Answer the questions about character development from pages 192–193 of** *Elisa's Diary*.

1. What does the author reveal about Elisa through her dialogue and her relationship with her brother?

_____

_____

_____

2. How can you tell that Elisa and her brother have different perspectives about their new home?

_____

_____

_____

▶ **Answer the questions about character development from pages 196–198.**

3. What does the author reveal about Elisa's perspective through her dialogue and relationship with José?

_____

_____

4. How does Elisa respond to challenges by the end of the story?

_____

_____

Name _____

Prefix semi–; Latin Roots scrib/script

The word *semicircle* contains the prefix *semi–* which means "half."

The words *scriptwriter* and *scribble* contain roots that have Latin origins. The meaning of the roots *script* and *scrib* is "write."

> Complete the chart with other words that contain the prefix *semi–* and the roots *scrib/script*.

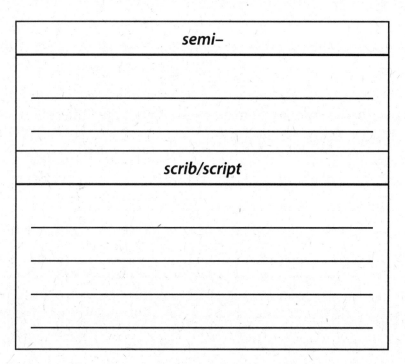

semi–
_____
_____
scrib/script
_____
_____
_____
_____

> Choose one word from each category and use it in a sentence.

_____

_____

_____

_____

Literary Elements

Literary elements are the parts that make up a story, such as characters, setting, and **plot**, including **conflict** and **resolution**. Many stories follow a chronological order, telling **events** in the order they happen. Sometimes, however, authors use the plot devices known as flashback and flash-forward. A flashback interrupts the story with an event from the past. A flash-forward interrupts the story with an event that will happen in the future. Both devices provide details that help the reader understand something important that is happening now.

> **Answer the questions about flashback from paragraphs 3–7 on pages 190–191 of** *Elisa's Diary*.

1. How does the author's use of flashback in these paragraphs help you understand what is happening now?

   _____

   _____

   _____

   _____

2. How does the author use the flashback to contrast the way Elisa felt then with the way she feels now?

   _____

   _____

   _____

   _____

Name _____

Final Stable Syllables –tion, –sion

▶ **Read each sentence. Then choose the word with the final stable syllable** _–tion_ **or** _–sion_ **from the word bank that best completes the sentence. Write the word in the blank.**

intrusion	direction	impression	equation
inclusion	description	depression	affection

1. It is always important to make a good first _____ .

2. Surpriya solved the difficult math _____.

3. A major economic downturn is called a _____ .

4. Please pardon my _____ into your private meeting.

5. Rey enjoyed the author's poetic _____ of the sunset.

6. Which _____ should I turn, left or right?

7. Jed had great _____ for the newborn puppy.

8. The _____ of young artists made the exhibit more exciting.

Name _____

Critical Vocabulary

You can use the words you learn from reading as you talk and write.

> Use what you learned about the vocabulary words from *Inside Out and Back Again* to support your answers to the questions below. Then use the Critical Vocabulary words as you talk with a partner about your answers.

1. Does the family's **sponsor** act out of **generosity,** or is there something else that motivates him? Explain.

_____

2. How can Hà show her mother that she feels **grateful**?

_____

3. What **goodwill** does Hà's family receive?

_____

4. Describe the rule and **exception** about the word *deer*.

_____

5. Does Hà think the rules of English are **sensible**? Explain.

_____

> **Choose two of the Critical Vocabulary words and use them in a sentence.**

_____

_____

_____

_____

Name _____

Elements of Poetry

Poetry looks different from other kinds of writing. The lines of a poem are shown in sections called **stanzas**. Poets use **figurative language** and **imagery**, or words that appeal to the senses, to create pictures in the minds of their readers and listeners. Figurative language and imagery help poets create mood and help readers share in poets' experiences and feelings.

Poets also use sound devices, such as **rhythm** and **repetition**, to create a mood or draw attention to an idea. Rhythm is a kind of beat, or meter. Certain syllables are stressed in each line of a poem to create a rhythmic pattern. Repetition is using the same word or sound over and over to show something is important or to add rhythm to the poem.

▶ **Answer the questions about elements of poetry on page 205 of** *Inside Out and Back Again*.

1. What mood does the poet create in "Out the Too-High Window"?

_____

_____

2. What words and phrases does the poet use to convey this mood?

_____

_____

_____

Name _____

Roots voc, ject

> Circle the Latin root in each word in the chart. Then complete the chart by looking up the meaning of each word using a print or online dictionary. Then write how the definition is connected to the root.

Word	Dictionary Definitions	Connection to Root
invocation		
vocalize		
conjecture		
dejected		

Theme

A **theme** is a lesson or message that an author wants to share with readers. Sometimes the theme is stated. Most often, however, the author does not directly state the theme but only implies it. Readers can figure out the theme by analyzing the text and asking questions about it. A poem usually has a single theme, and a certain phrase or sentence, or even a repeated word, can reveal that poem's theme. With a collection of poems, the poems all may relate to the same theme in some way.

▶ **Answer the questions about theme on pages 205–209 of** *Inside Out and Back Again.*

1. What challenges does the speaker face?

_____

_____

2. What feelings does the speaker express about her new life in the United States?

_____

_____

3. What lesson or message is the poet developing in these first few poems?

_____

_____

▶ **Answer these questions about theme on page 214.**

4. How does Hà feel about school and living in the United States in "Someone Knows" and "Most Relieved Day"? Why does she feel like this?

_____

_____

5. What message, or theme, does the poet develop in these poems?

_____

_____

Name _____

Final Stable Syllables –tion, –sion

▶ **Read each sentence. Then underline the correct spelling of the word ending in** –tion **or** –sion **that completes the sentence.**

1. Alexis picked up a _____ at the pharmacy.

   prescription   prescribtion

2. The football star suffered a _____ when he was tackled.

   concussion   concustion

3. Syed asked his grandmother for _____ to attend the party.

   permition   permission

4. The smallest town in the county had a _____ of 312 people.

   populatetion   population

5. There's a _____ of train service because of the snowstorm.

   suspension   suspendsion

6. In the news, we read about the volcanic _____ .

   erupttion   eruption

7. Chen made a _____ to Dr. Medoza's research.

   contribution   contribusion

8. This movie features a lot of dramatic _____ .

   tenseion   tension

Name _____

Text and Graphic Features

Text features can help readers understand the important parts of a story. For example, headings can show chapter or section breaks. Different typefaces can show emphasis or indicate a title. **Graphic features**, which are visuals such as illustrations or maps, also connect readers to a story by explaining or illustrating different parts of the story. Illustrations can further connect readers to the characters and setting by showing readers an artist's version of what the characters and setting might look like. Illustrations also help create tone and contribute to the beauty of the text.

▶ **Answer the questions about text and graphic features on pages 212–213 of** *Inside Out and Back Again.*

1. What do the pictures on these pages show?

_____

_____

_____

_____

_____

2. What does the picture reveal about how Hà feels when she is learning English?

_____

_____

_____

_____

Name _____

Prefixes com-, con-, pre-, pro-

▶ **Read each sentence and look for the word that contains the prefix** *com-*, *con-*, *pre-*, **or** *pro-*. **Write the word on the line after the sentence, and divide the word after the prefix.**

1. *Sunflower* and *moonlight* are examples of compound words.

_____

2. This movie about wizards will really appeal to the preteen crowd.

_____

3. One example of a pronoun is *she*.

_____

4. After the bridge is built, it will connect these two cities.

_____

5. I like to premix all my paint colors before I begin painting.

_____

6. Can you run this program on your laptop?

_____

7. If we combine our money, we will have enough to buy this game.

_____

8. Don't forget to preheat the oven before you make the batter.

_____

Name _____

Critical Vocabulary

You can use the words you learn from reading as you talk and write.

▶ Use details from *Mr. Linden's Library* to support your answers to the activity below. Read each sentence. Underline the sentence that best fits the meaning of the word in dark print. Then use the Critical Vocabulary words as you talk with a partner about your answers.

1. engulfed

The rising river flooded the whole town.
Heavy rain pelted the town for several days.

2. audible

Mr. Linden made tea in the kitchen downstairs.
Carol could hear the clink of the teakettle.

3. relentlessly

A gust of wind blew through the open window.
The harsh wind blew all night long without stopping.

4. prefer

Coffee? No thanks. I would rather have a cup of tea.
Amelia ordered a cup of tea with her muffin.

5. keepsake

I wear the gold pin Aunt Lil gave me to remind me of her.
I wore a beautiful gold pin when we visited Aunt Lil.

6. will

A dealer offered to purchase all of Mr. Linden's books.
After his death, he wanted his money given to charity.

7. sentimental

Theo liked riding on the train to work every day.
Theo kept some of the toy trains he had as a child.

Name _____

8. formidable

Their undefeated team would be difficult to beat.

I practiced kicking the soccer ball every afternoon.

9. musings

He likes to go to the park and play with his friends.

He sat under a tree all day and let his mind wander.

▶ **Choose two of the Critical Vocabulary words and use them in a sentence.**

_____

_____

_____

_____

Name _____

Characters

A **character** is a person (or animal) in a story. Authors bring their characters to life by including dialogue and by describing each character's appearance, traits, behaviors, thoughts, and emotions. Authors sometimes develop characters by describing interactions, relationships, and conflicts with other characters.

▶ **Answer the questions from page 237 of *Mr. Linden's Library*.**

1. How would you describe Carol?

_____

_____

2. How are Carol and Mr. Linden alike?

_____

3. How does Carol respond to a tea invitation? What does this show about her perspective?

_____

_____

▶ **Now answer these questions from page 243.**

4. How does the author reveal Carol's and Mr. Linden's different perspectives about the mysterious book?

_____

_____

5. How does Mr. Linden react when Carol asks about the mysterious book he's reading?

_____

_____

6. How does this interaction add to the story's conflict?

_____

_____

Name _____

Prefixes com–, con–, pre–, pro–

▶ **Choose the word from the box that best fits each definition. Write the word on the line.**

combine	prohibit	prepare	connection	consume
proceed	preapprove	compare	profession	predict

1. _____ to put things together to see how they are the same

2. _____ to go forward or onward

3. _____ to get ready for something or to get something ready

4. _____ to put things together

5. _____ to say what will happen before it occurs

6. _____ to forbid or make impossible

7. _____ to eat or drink something

8. _____ an occupation or career

9. _____ a link between persons, things, or ideas

10. _____ to give permission in advance

Name _____

Latin Roots *fac, fec, fy*

The words *factor*, *effect*, and *falsify* contain Latin roots. The roots *fac* and *fec* mean "do or make." The root *fy* means "to make."

▶ **Complete the chart with other words that contain the Latin roots *fac*, *fec*, and *fy*.**

fac	*fec*	*fy*
_____	_____	_____
_____	_____	_____
_____	_____	_____

▶ **Choose one word from each category and use it in a sentence.**

_____

_____

_____

_____

_____

_____

_____

_____

_____

_____

_____

_____

Name _____

Literary Elements

Story structure refers to what happens in a story and when and how things happen. It includes **plot, conflict, rising action, climax, falling action,** and **resolution.**

> **Answer the questions on pages 238–239 of *Mr. Linden's Library*.**

1. What does Carol notice about Mr. Linden's book?

_____

_____

_____

_____

2. What problem does Carol want to solve?

_____

_____

_____

_____

3. How does she try to solve the problem?

_____

_____

_____

_____

Name _____

Figurative Language

When writing a story, authors choose their words carefully to establish the mood and to help readers visualize and experience the events and characters in the story. **Figurative language** compares two things by using words and expressions that typically mean something different from their dictionary definitions. **Imagery** uses **sensory words** to appeal to readers' senses and help them feel what characters feel.

> **Answer the questions from page 232 of *Mr. Linden's Library*.**

1. Which words and phrases help you picture Josiah Linden's house?

_____

_____

_____

2. What kind of mood do these words and phrases establish?

_____

_____

> **Answer these additional questions from page 234.**

3. In paragraph 17, what are some of the sensory words and phrases that help you picture what Carol experiences as she enters Mr. Linden's library?

_____

_____

_____

4. How does this description of the inside of Mr. Linden's home compare with the description of his home at the beginning of the story?

_____

_____

_____

Name _____

Suffixes –ant, –ent, –able, –ible, –ism, –ist

> **Read each sentence. Find the words that have the suffixes** *–ant, –ent, –able, –ible,* *–ism,* **and** *–ist.* **Underline the suffixes.**

1. It will be tolerable for you to miss the next meeting.

2. There is insufficient information to be able to make a decision.

3. This burnt cake is entirely inedible!

4. The teacher offered constructive criticism for each student's essay.

5. I don't think Miguel is very comfortable in that shirt.

6. Steve planned to hire a new assistant as soon as possible.

7. Jamal knew that he wanted to be a scientist someday.

8. Kelly was unsure if her new car would be reliable in the snow.

Name _____

Critical Vocabulary

You can use the words you learn from reading as you talk and write.

> Use details from *The Loch Ness Monster* to support your answers to the activity below. Read each sentence. Underline the sentence that best fits the meaning of the word in dark print. Then use the Critical Vocabulary words as you talk with a partner about your answers.

1. sightings

Each morning on my walk, the birds fly from tree to tree.
I did not see any birds on my walk today.

2. chastised

The girl received an award for her good behavior.
The girl was sent to the principal's office for being rude to other students.

3. desperately

He begged and pleaded with his parents to buy a new computer.
He was very happy with the computer he received for his birthday.

4. convinced

After talking to her for an hour, I realized that her opinion was correct.
I would not change my mind even after an hour-long discussion.

5. earnest

She had a lot of passion when she talked about her favorite restaurant.
She did not care one way or another about which restaurant they went to.

> Choose two of the Critical Vocabulary words and use them in a sentence.

_____

_____

_____

_____

Name _____

Media Techniques

Media are the ways in which ideas can be communicated, such as through books, film, television, and the Internet. **Media techniques**, including various visual and sound elements, are tools media creators use to help their audiences better understand the information and ideas presented.

▶ **Answer the questions about reenactment and live-action video in** *The Loch Ness Monster*.

1. What places does the live-action video show?

_____

_____

_____

_____

2. What real-life people and events do actors portray?

_____

_____

_____

_____

3. How do reenactments and live-action video help you understand how the "surgeon's photo" was made in 1934?

_____

_____

_____

Suffixes –ant, –ent, –able, –ible, –ism, –ist

▶ In each sentence, there is a word that needs a suffix. Choose a suffix from the box that will complete the word and make sense in the sentence.

–ant	–ent	–able	–ible	–ism	–ist

1. The accident was entirely unavoid_____ .

2. Maria was excited to be a final_____ in the spelling contest.

3. The smell of those muffins baking is totally irresist_____ .

4. The occup_____ of this apartment is required to keep it clean.

5. Derek became more independ_____ when he went away to college.

6. Her daughter imitated her manner_____ of talking with her hands.

7. Please make a sens_____ choice for lunch today.

8. Teachers should treat students equally and not show favorit_____ .

Name _____

Critical Vocabulary

You can use the words you learn from reading as you talk and write.

▶ **Use what you know about the vocabulary words from *Finding Bigfoot* to help you finish each sentence. Then use the Critical Vocabulary words as you talk with a partner about your answers.**

1. To avoid dangerous **encounters** with wildlife . . .

_____

2. When I was younger, I had a **misperception** that . . .

_____

3. Scientists can test a **theoretical** idea by . . .

_____

4. Panthers are **elusive** creatures because . . .

_____

5. **Hoaxes** are never a good idea because . . .

_____

▶ **Choose two of the Critical Vocabulary words and use them in a sentence.**

_____

_____

_____

Name _____

Ideas and Support

In some informational texts, an author may try to influence readers to think a certain way. Authors may use **facts** or **opinions** in expressing their ideas. Identifying an author's ideas as facts or opinions and evaluating the **evidence** the author uses to support those ideas can help readers better understand a text and decide whether they agree with the author.

▶ **Answer these questions about the section "The Case for Cryptids" on page 259 of** *Finding Bigfoot.*

1. Why is the phrase "the case for" in the heading a clue about the author's opinion on cryptids, or hidden animals?

   _____

   _____

   _____

   _____

2. What opinions go against the idea that cryptids exist? Cite text evidence to support your response.

   _____

   _____

   _____

   _____

3. What facts does the author use to support the claim that cryptids exist?

   _____

   _____

   _____

   _____

Name _____

Suffixes –y, –ion, –ic, –ous, –less

The suffix –y means "chacterized by," –ion means "action," –ic means "relating to," –ous means "full of," and –less means "without."

▸ Complete the chart with other words that contain the suffixes –y, –ion, –ic, –ous, –less.

–y	–ion	–ic
_____	_____	_____
_____	_____	_____
_____	_____	_____
–ous	**–less**	
_____	_____	
_____	_____	
_____	_____	

▸ Choose one word from each category and use it in a sentence.

_____

_____

_____

_____

_____

_____

_____

_____

Name _____

Text and Graphic Features

Authors use **text features**, such as headings, punctuation, and boldfaced words, to draw attention to specific parts of a text and to help readers find information. They use **graphic features**, such as illustrations, **diagrams**, and maps, to explain ideas in the text in a visual way or to add information related to the ideas in the text. Using a text and its features together helps readers gain a clearer or deeper understanding of the author's ideas.

▶ **Answer the questions about the text features on pages 262–263 of *Finding Bigfoot*.**

1. What does the main heading "The Arguments for Bigfoot" tell you about this section?

_____

_____

_____

_____

2. How do the section's four subheadings help readers?

_____

_____

_____

_____

3. Why do you think the author organizes the text this way?

_____

_____

_____

_____

Name _____

Greek Word Roots

▶ **Each sentence contains an incomplete word. Choose a Greek root from the box to complete the word. Look at the boldfaced word in the sentence for a clue. Word roots may be used more than once.**

bio	micro	photo
graph	phone	phon

1. A _____graphy tells the story of a person's **life**.

2. Words or other materials printed on _____film look very **small**.

3. If you wear ear_____s, you can hear the **sound** in your ears.

4. A substance that reacts to **light** can be said to be _____active.

5. My mother plays **violin** in the local sym_____y.

6. The teacher asked us to **write** the sources we quote in a biblio_____y.

7. A _____copier uses **light** and electricity to reproduce a printed image.

8. Fossils vary in size from giant bones to very **small** _____fossils.

Name _____

Critical Vocabulary

You can use the words you learn from reading as you talk and write.

> Use what you learned about the vocabulary words from *The Secret Keepers* to help you answer the questions. Then use the Critical Vocabulary words as you talk with a partner about your answers.

1. What does Reuben do that causes light to be **extinguished**?

_____

2. What details about the watch **beckoned** Reuben to discover its secrets?

_____

3. What surprise left Reuben **gaping** at his mother?

_____

4. Why might a **muffled** sound be frightening to Reuben?

_____

5. Does Reuben work **hastily** to unlock the watch? How do you know?

_____

6. Why does Reuben's **conviction** about setting the watch to 12 give him a **shudder**?

_____

7. How does Reuben's **faltering** voice show how he feels about what the watch can do?

_____

Name _____

8. What events in the story leave Reuben feeling **feeble**?

_____

▶ **Choose two of the Critical Vocabulary words and use them in a sentence.**

_____

_____

_____

_____

Literary Elements

Literary elements are the pieces that make up a story. They include characters, setting, **plot**, and **events**. A story's plot has conflict (the problems the characters face) and resolution (how the problems are solved). The events, however, are the things that happen in the story that change the character, affect the mood, or build the plot's conflict and resolution. Sometimes authors may slow down or speed up scenes or events in a story to move the plot along and create a specific mood.

▶ **Answer these questions about literary elements from page 276 of** *The Secret Keepers.*

1. Does the author slow down or speed up the pacing of events in paragraphs 15–16? How can you tell?

   _____

   _____

   _____

   _____

2. How does changing the pace of events in this scene impact the plot?

   _____

   _____

   _____

   _____

Name _____

Review Suffixes -ous/-ious, -ant, -ment

> Complete the chart with four words with suffixes *–ous/–ious, –ant,* or *–ment*. Write each word in the first column and underline the suffix. Write the definition of the suffix in the second column. Next, predict each word's definition. Then, look up the definition of the word to confirm your predictions.

Word	Suffix Definition	Predicted Definition	Dictionary Definition of Word
1.			
2.			
3.			
4.			

Author's Craft

A story's **mood** describes the emotions and feelings of readers while they read the story. **Tone** is an author's attitude toward the characters, subject, or audience. Authors choose certain words and phrases to create tone and mood in a mystery.

> **Answer these questions about author's craft from page 275 of *The Secret Keepers*.**

1. What words and phrases help you picture how Reuben feels as he tries the watch-winding experiment?

   _____

   _____

   _____

   _____

2. What type of mood do these word choices create?

   _____

   _____

> **Answer these additional questions about tone and mood from page 283.**

3. What words and phrases are repeated in paragraphs 46–51?

   _____

   _____

   _____

4. How does the author's use of repetition impact the story?

   _____

5. How does the tense mood contribute to the story's theme?

   _____

   _____

Name _____

Greek Word Roots

▶ Read each definition. Then write the word from the box that matches the definition on the line.

telegram	phonograph	dialogue	biofuel
micrography	photographer	microbiologist	periscope

1. words spoken between two people

   _____

2. a machine that plays "written" sounds from a record

   _____

3. a person who makes pictures by "writing" with light

   _____

4. a message sent by wires to a faraway place

   _____

5. a person who studies tiny life forms

   _____

6. energy made from matter that was once alive

   _____

7. writing in very small letters

   _____

8. a device for viewing things that are not in a direct line of sight

   _____

Name _____

Point of View

The **point of view** of a story refers to the **narrator**, or the person who is telling the story. In some stories, the narrator is a character in the story who describes events from his or her perspective and speaks about his or her actions and thoughts using the pronouns *I*, *mine*, and *me*. This is called first-person point of view. When the narrator is outside the story, the point of view is called third-person point of view. A third-person narrator might know what each character does, feels, and knows, as well as everything that happens in the story.

▶ **Answer these questions about point of view from page 272 of *The Secret Keepers*.**

1. What point of view does the author use in this story? How do you know?

_____

_____

_____

_____

2. How might this story be different if it were told from Reuben's point of view?

_____

_____

_____

_____

Name _____

Latin Word Roots

> Read each definition. Then add the correct Latin word root from the word bank to complete the word being defined. Latin word roots may be used more than once.

port	dict
rupt	spect

1. _____er: a person who carries travelers' bags

2. _____ate: to say something that another person will write down

3. cor_____: having broken or destroyed morals

4. _____age: the act of carrying boats between two bodies of water

5. _____ator: a person who watches an event

6. _____acle: something amazing that can be seen

7. dis_____: to break apart the way something normally works

8. _____ionary: a book that shows how words are said and what they mean

Critical Vocabulary

You can use the words you learn from reading as you talk and write.

▶ **Use details from *Willie B.* to support your answers to the activity below. Read each sentence. Underline the sentence that best fits the meaning of the word in dark print. Then use the Critical Vocabulary words as you talk with a partner about your answers.**

1. solitary

She likes to paint but also likes drawing and sketching.
She spends many hours alone each day, drawing and sketching.

2. dominated

From the start, the Tigers showed they were the stronger team.
Before the season, the Tigers practiced their plays every day.

3. enclosure

Lambs can wiggle out through a hole in the fence.
The farmer built a new pen for the sheep and lambs.

4. anticipation

I couldn't sit still because I was excited for the show to start.
I didn't pay attention to the show because I was sleepy.

5. inhumane

The thin, hungry animals were crowded into a small space.
The animals were different from any others I had seen.

6. coaxing

Stuck high in the tree, the kitten was crying loudly.
I tried to get the kitten inside the house by offering it a treat.

7. generation

He prefers spending most of his time alone.
He has a lot in common with other people his own age.

Name _____

8. possession

This necklace is the most precious thing I own.

My sister said I can borrow her necklace for the party.

9. territory

The children keep their pet rabbits in a cage in their backyard.

Rabbits spend their whole lives in an area of ten acres or less.

> **Choose two of the Critical Vocabulary words and use them in a sentence.**

_____

_____

_____

_____

Name _____

Theme

The **theme** of a selection is the main message, moral, or lesson that the author wants readers to learn. Readers often must figure out the theme of a text based on the author's word choice and phrasing, together with the events and other details the author chooses to include.

> **Answer these questions about theme from page 302 of** *Willie B.: A Story of Hope*.

1. What theme is developed in these paragraphs?

_____

_____

2. What details support this theme?

_____

_____

_____

> **Answer these additional questions about theme from page 308.**

3. What happens in paragraph 19?

_____

_____

4. When Willie B. runs to the top of the hill, what does this say about him?

_____

_____

5. What theme can you identify based on the events?

_____

_____

_____

Name _____

Latin Word Roots

▶ Read the information in each chart. Then put together the Latin root, prefix, and suffix to form the word with the meaning shown. Write the word on the blank line.

1.

Root	Prefix	Suffix	Meaning
rupt	inter	ed	broke into or between

Word: _____

2.

Root	Prefix	Suffix	Meaning
dict	bene	ion	a spoken blessing or expression of good wishes

Word: _____

3.

Root	Prefix	Suffix	Meaning
port	trans	ed	carried across

Word: _____

4.

Root	Prefix	Suffix	Meaning
rupt	dis	ive	causing confusion or disorder

Word: _____

5.

Root	Prefix	Suffix	Meaning
spect	intro	ive	looking into one's own thoughts and feelings

Word: _____

6.

Root	Prefix	Suffix	Meaning
spect	pro	ive	looking forward

Word: _____

7.

Root	Prefix	Suffix	Meaning
dict	contra	ion	something that states the opposite of what is true

Word: _____

Name _____

Review Prefixes

The words *inhumane*, *antisocial*, and *predominate* contain the prefixes *in–*, *anti–*, and *pre–*.
Other examples of prefixes include *re–*, *ex–*, *un–*, and *dis–*.

> Complete the chart with words from *Willie B.* that contain the following prefixes.

re–	
ex–	
un–	
dis–	
pre–	

> Write a sentence for each word in the chart.

_____

_____

_____

_____

_____

_____

_____

_____

_____

_____

_____

_____

_____

_____

Name _____

Author's Craft

An author's **tone** reveals how the author feels about a subject. Tone is revealed through the author's word choice, phrasing, and attention to the subject's experiences and feelings.

▶ **Answer the questions from page 307 of *Willie B.: A Story of Hope*.**

1. What words would you use to describe the author's tone toward Willie B. and his new situation?

   _____

   _____

   _____

   _____

2. Which sentences have words and/or details that best show the tone in paragraph 17?

   _____

   _____

   _____

   _____

3. How does the author's tone in this section affect the theme of the selection?

   _____

   _____

   _____

   _____

Name _____

Text Structure

Text structure is the way a text is arranged to help readers understand the information. Authors use the **compare and contrast** text structure to show how things are alike and different.

> ▶ **Answer the questions from page 304 of** *Willie B.: A Story of Hope.*

1. How does the author use compare and contrast to show how Willie B. is similar to and different from a person?

   _____

   _____

   _____

   _____

2. What do you learn about Willie B. from this part of the text?

   _____

   _____

   _____

   _____

> ▶ **Answer the questions from pages 306–307.**

3. What major change did Dr. Maple make to the zoo when he became director?

   _____

   _____

   _____

4. How do you think changing the name of the zoo made it a better place?

   _____

   _____

Name _____

Suffixes –ion, –ation

▶ In each sentence, there is a word with the suffix *–ion* or *–ation*. Identify the root word and write it on the blank line.

1. The preservation of animal habitats is important.

   root word: _____

2. My reflection in this very old mirror is wavy.

   root word: _____

3. The vet will give my gerbil an examination.

   root word: _____

4. He was disappointed to receive a rejection from his first choice of colleges.

   root word: _____

5. Have you memorized all of your subtraction facts?

   root word: _____

6. The town has a population of 675 people.

   root word: _____

7. Did she give you any indication as to when she will arrive?

   root word: _____

8. We need the person who broke the lamp to make a confession.

   root word: _____

Name _____

Critical Vocabulary

You can use the words you learn from reading as you talk and write.

▶ **Use details and ideas from** *National Geographic: Dolphin Parenting* **to help you answer the questions. Then use the Critical Vocabulary words as you talk with a partner about your answers.**

1. Why does a young dolphin mimic a mother's **posture**?

_____

2. What skills can a dolphin **utilize** to find food?

_____

3. What problems would a young dolphin have if it had to **fend** for itself?

_____

4. What skill gives a dolphin **status** with other dolphins?

_____

5. What can a dolphin that has **mastered** hydroplaning find?

_____

6. What **technique** is most important for dolphins to learn?

_____

▶ **Choose two of the Critical Vocabulary words and use them in a sentence.**

_____

_____

_____

_____

Name _____

Media Techniques

Media techniques are tools that help communicate ideas and meaning to **media** audiences. These can include visual and sound elements. Media techniques help viewers better understand the topic's concepts and how ideas are related.

▶ **Answer the questions about the effectiveness of media techniques in** *Dolphin Parenting.*

1. Are the techniques used in *Dolphin Parenting* effective? Why?

_____

_____

_____

_____

2. What is the video's overall message? Why is it effective?

_____

_____

_____

_____

Suffixes –ion, –ation

> Read each sentence. Beneath each sentence, there is a root word. Add the correct suffix to the root word and write it in the blank.

1. The _____ on his knee was very effective.

root word: operate

2. The doctor treated the _____ with an antibiotic.

root word: infect

3. Did you attend the New Year's _____ ?

root word: celebrate

4. When people act in _____, they do not function well.

root word: desperate

5. By the time I finished the race, I was covered with _____ .

root word: perspire

6. Listen to this _____, and write down what you hear.

root word: dictate

7. Her _____ to succeed will influence her future.

root word: determine

8. Make a _____ about what you think will happen next.

root word: predict

Name _____

Critical Vocabulary

You can use the words you learn from reading as you talk and write.

> **Use details from *Can We Be Friends* to support your answers to the activity below. Read each sentence. Underline the sentence that best fits the meaning of the word in dark print. Then use the Critical Vocabulary words as you talk with a partner about your answers.**

1. reconcile

Todd and Julia could work together again after he said he was sorry.

Todd and Julia just met, but they agreed to work on the project.

2. benefit

The zoo is open from 10:00 a.m.–5:00 p.m. daily.

The new hours will allow you to visit the zoo more often.

3. restore

We will get power back as soon as the fallen wires are fixed.

The ice and snow caused the power to go out.

4. cowered

The frightened puppy hid behind its mother.

The puppy slept in the sun after a long walk.

5. clan

Family members from all over the country came to our reunion.

Friends and neighbors will gather for a block party on Sunday.

6. enabled

Thanks to a successful fundraiser, our class went on a field trip.

Our field trip included a visit to a museum and a park.

> **Choose two of the Critical Vocabulary words and use them in a sentence.**

_____

_____

Name _____

Central Idea

The **central idea** of a text is what the text is mostly about. Relevant **details** provide information about the central idea. Typical relevant details include facts, examples, statistics, reasons, or definitions. To determine the central idea of a text or a section of a text, readers look at the details carefully. Then they ask themselves what idea all the details tell about.

> Answer the question about the central idea on page 326 of *Can We Be Friends?*

1. What is the central idea?

_____

_____

_____

> Answer this question about the central idea on page 328.

2. What is the central idea?

_____

_____

_____

> Answer this additional question about the central idea.

3. What is the central idea of the entire selection, *Can We Be Friends?*

_____

_____

_____

_____

_____

Name _____

Latin Root bene

The word *benefit* contains a root that has Latin origins. The meaning of the root *bene* is "good."

> **Complete the chart with words that contain the root *bene*.**

bene
_____
_____

> **Use each word in a sentence.**

_____

_____

_____

_____

Name _____

Text Structure

Authors organize information in a way that helps readers see how ideas are connected. The way a text is organized is called its **text structure**. Authors may use one text structure or a variety of structures in a text, depending on their purpose and the information they are presenting. In a problem/solution structure, the author explains a problem and then tells how it is resolved, or fixed. In a cause/effect structure, the author explains what happened and why it happened. In a sequence of events structure, the author shows events or steps in order. In a compare/contrast structure, the author shows how two or more things are alike and different.

▷ **Answer the questions about text structure on page 326 of** *Can We Be Friends?*

1. How are the ideas on page 326 organized?

_____

_____

2. How do you know?

_____

_____

_____

_____

_____

_____

▷ **Answer this additional question about text structure on page 327.**

3. What text structures are used in paragraph 13?

_____

_____

_____

Name _____

Final Stable Syllables with /ər/

> Read each sentence. Then underline the correct spelling of the word with a final /ər/ syllable to complete the sentence.

1. The police caught the _____ and returned the stolen goods.

        burglor   burglar

2. On hot summer days, Jakhil and Elle played in the _____ .

        sprinkler   sprinklar

3. The young _____ played a leading role in the play.

        actor   acter

4. Grace took her jacket to a _____ to be repaired.

        tailer   tailor

5. Just _____ if you need anything.

        holler   hollar

6. The wall was made of brick and _____ .

        mortor   mortar

7. We can overcome this _____ obstacle.

        minar   minor

8. The _____ president gave a speech at graduation.

        former   formor

Name _____

Critical Vocabulary

You can use the words you learn from reading as you talk and write.

> **Use what you learned about the vocabulary words from *Winter Bees* to help you finish each sentence. Then use the Critical Vocabulary words as you talk with a partner about your answers.**

1. We watched **formations** of . . .

_____

2. I looked at **random** magazines to . . .

_____

3. I had to **grasp** the handle to . . .

_____

4. Some birds **migrate** because . . .

_____

5. I **scaled** the steps to . . .

_____

6. An **aquatic** pet needs . . .

_____

7. I am **resistant** to the idea of . . .

_____

8. One day I will **resume** my . . .

_____

> **Choose two of the Critical Vocabulary words and use them in a sentence.**

_____

_____

Theme

The **theme** of a story or text is the main message, lesson, or moral that the author wants readers to know. Typically, a theme can be expressed in one sentence. Sometimes an author clearly states the theme. Sometimes it's implied, or suggested, and the reader must figure it out using details in the text. When a theme is implied, one way to figure it out is to ask yourself, "What is the author trying to teach me?"

> Answer the question about theme on pages 334 and 336 of *Winter Bees and Other Poems of the Cold.*

1. What is one theme that is developed in both "Dream of the Tundra Swan" and "Snake's Lullaby"?

   _____

   _____

   _____

> Answer these additional questions on page 340.

2. What theme is introduced in the first stanza of "Winter Bees"?

   _____

   _____

   _____

   _____

3. Where else in the poem is this theme developed?

   _____

   _____

   _____

   _____

Name _____

Review Roots

> Predict the definition of each word. Next look up the definition to confirm your predictions.

ROOT: Definition	Word	Predicted Definition	Dictionary Definition of Word
1. *bene*: good	benedictory		
2. *ject*: throw	projectile		
3. *auto*: self	autocrat		
4. *bio*: life	biohazard		

> Choose two words and write a sentence for each.

_____

_____

_____

_____

_____

Name _____

Text and Graphic Features

Informational texts often have **text features** (such as bold text, headings, and glossaries) and **graphic features** (such as diagrams, illustrations, graphs, charts, maps, and timelines) to help explain the information in the text.

▶ **Answer the questions on page 339 of** *Winter Bees and Other Poems of the Cold.*

1. According to the text, what are snowflakes?

_____

_____

_____

2. Why are snowflakes different from each other?

_____

_____

_____

3. How does the illustration support the text?

_____

_____

_____

4. What is another idea in the text that is supported by the illustration?

_____

_____

_____

Final Stable Syllables with /ər/

▶ Read each sentence. From the chart of words containing the final stable syllable /ər/, choose the word that best completes the sentence and write it in the blank.

barrier	escalator	unpopular	protractor
maneuver	constrictor	particular	editor

1. Would you rather take the stairs or the _____ to the second floor?

2. This _____ will block the dog from leaving the yard.

3. Guy used his _____ to measure the angle.

4. Aja had many friends and was never _____ .

5. Ms. Mendoza was very _____ about how to solve equations.

6. The surprise attack required a complicated military _____ .

7. The magazine's _____ accepted Cesar's story.

8. Farah decided to get a pet iguana rather than a boa _____ .

Name _____

Author's Craft

Author's craft refers to the language and techniques an author uses to make his or her writing interesting and to communicate ideas to the reader. One way writers use author's craft is through their word choice, which includes the author's general vocabulary and use of precise nouns, sensory words, and vivid verbs that make the text engaging. Authors also use figurative language (words that mean something different from their dictionary definitions) and imagery (word choices that help create images in a reader's mind).

> **Answer the questions about "Snake's Lullaby" from pages 336–337 of *Winter Bees and Other Poems of the Cold*.**

1. How does the poet use figurative language to describe the snakes' actions?

_____

_____

_____

_____

2. How does the description in paragraph 11 support and explain the ideas in the poem?

_____

_____

_____

_____

3. How does the poet use figurative language to describe how winter affects snakes?

_____

_____

_____

_____

Name _____

Recognize Root Words with Spelling Changes

➤ **Read each sentence and note the word in bold. Then complete the sentence by writing the correct root word of the word in bold.**

1. Jay worried the shirt would not _____, but the **fitted** shirt was a perfect size.

2. The spray **repelled** the mosquitos, but it did not _____ the flies.

3. He **inferred** one motive, but she did not _____ the same motive.

4. If you don't have a _____, you are not **permitted** to drive.

5. After **stripping** the paint off the chair, you should _____ the table.

6. Maria was **strapping** on a new _____ because the old one had broken.

7. Left untreated, the **recurring** pain will _____ for the rest of your life.

8. Stop **referring** to the dog as "sweetie"—that's how you _____ to me!

Name _____

Recognize Root Words with Spelling Changes

▶ **Read each sentence. Underline the word in the sentence whose root has a spelling change caused by its suffix. Then write the root word on the blank below.**

1. The student was compelled to retake the course she failed.

   root word: _____

2. The doctor's office was not equipped with an x-ray machine.

   root word: _____

3. Ankit remitted the payment by mail.

   root word: _____

4. The plumber unstopped the drain.

   root word: _____

5. Tom was propelling the boat forward with the oars.

   root word: _____

6. Angela was eavesdropping when she overheard the secret.

   root word: _____

7. Enrique decided that scrapping the plan was the best option.

   root word: _____

8. His mom permitted Daniel to stay up late last night.

   root word: _____

Words from Other Languages

> Read each sentence and look at the underlined word. Use a print or online dictionary that shows pronunciations to look up the word. Circle the answer that shows how the underlined word is pronounced.

1. A buffet is a table from which meals or refreshments are served.

bə-fā   bə-fĕt

2. A wallet is a pocket-sized folding case that holds money.

wă-lā   wŏl-ĭt

3. Crochet is a form of needlework that uses hooked needles.

krō-shā   krō-shĕt

4. A chauffeur drives other people, usually in a fancy car.

chō-fər   shō-fər

5. A chandelier is a decorative light fixture hung from the ceiling.

chan-də-lîr   shăn-də-lîr

6. To chasten means to correct or discipline by punishment.

chā-sən   shā-sən

7. A plague is a highly infectious disease epidemic.

plāg   plāg-wā

8. To segue is to transition to another part of a piece of music.

sĕg   sĕg-wā

9. An epilogue is a concluding section at the end of a work of literature.

ĕp-ə-lôg   ĕp-ə-lôg-wā

Words from Other Languages

▶ Read each sentence and look at the underlined word. Use a print or online dictionary to look up the word. Circle the answer that shows how the underlined word is pronounced.

1. Collage is a French word. A collage is a compilation of materials pasted on a surface.

     kō-läzh   kō-lŏj

2. Armada is a Spanish word. An armada is a fleet of warships.

     är-mă-dă   är-mä-də

3. Premiere is a French word. A premiere is the first performance of a play or movie.

     prĭ-mî-âr   prĭ-mîr

4. Guacamole is a Spanish word. Guacamole is a dip made of mashed avocado.

     gwŏk-ə-mō-lē   gwŏk-ə-mōl

5. Depot is a French word. A depot is a railroad or bus station.

     dē-pō   dē-pŏt

6. Tortilla is a Spanish word. A tortilla is a flat disk of bread, usually made of corn or flour.

     tôr-tē-yə   tôr-tĭl-ə

7. Umbrella is an Italian word. An umbrella provides protection from rain.

     ŭm-brĕ-yə   ŭm-brĕl-ə

8. Garage is a French word. A garage is an indoor place to keep your car.

     gə-räzh   gə-rĭj

9. Garbage is not a word taken from another language. Garbage is a synonym of *trash*.

     gər-bäzh   gär-bĭj

Name _____

Adding Suffixes

▶ **Read each sentence. Find the words that have the suffixes. Underline the suffixes.**

1. The rough rope irritated my skin.

2. I retraced my route to find where I had lost my key.

3. The engagement party for the couple had a buffet.

4. If you work hard, you will see an improvement in your grades.

5. The hood on the coat is removable.

6. The story about the lost dog was very believable.

7. The child secretly took an extra cookie.

8. She was remorseful about her past mistakes.

Name _____

Adding Suffixes

▶ Read each sentence with a blank, and then look at the base word and suffix listed below it. Write the base word with the suffix added in the blank.

1. The drought caused a _____ of food.

   Base word and suffix: scarce + –ness

2. I was touched by the _____ of her apology.

   Base word and suffix: sincere + –ness

3. The two shirts are similar, and their prices are _____.

   Base word and suffix: compare + –able

4. The messy kitchen is in _____ condition.

   Base word and suffix: deplore + –able

5. The library is _____ important old documents.

   Base word and suffix: preserve + –ing

6. I am _____ between wearing my gym shoes and my sandals.

   Base word and suffix: alternate + –ing

7. Everyone was saddened by the _____ tragedy.

   Base word and suffix: sense + –less

8. The car's new engine was almost _____.

   Base word and suffix: noise + –less

Adding Suffixes –ent/–ence/–ency, –ant/–ance/–ancy

> **Read each sentence. Beneath each sentence are related words with different suffixes. Write the word with the suffix that correctly completes the sentence. If you are unsure which word is correct, consult a dictionary.**

1. Rachel is _____ to sing in front of others.

     reluctant   reluctance

2. David agreed to do it but with great _____.

     reluctant   reluctance

3. Once you have more experience, you will gain _____.

     confident   confidence

4. I am _____ you will succeed.

     confident   confidence

5. Mei likes the _____ of that perfume.

     fragrant   fragrance

6. That bouquet is very _____.

     fragrant   fragrance

7. Tyler gets _____ grades but could probably do better.

     decent   decency

8. Everyone deserves to be treated with _____.

     decent   decency

Adding Suffixes -ent/-ence/-ency, -ant/-ance/-ancy

> Read each sentence below and the suffixes listed beneath them. Write the suffix that correctly completes the sentence in the blank. If you are unsure which suffix is correct, consult a dictionary.

1. The patient is depend_____ on a life-support system.

    –ent   –ence   –ency

2. The colonies won independ_____ from Britain.

    –ent   –ence   –ency

3. Let's meet at a conveni_____ place.

    –ent   –ence   –ency

4. When training a dog, consist_____ is important.

    –ent   –ence   –ency

5. I have a tend_____ to forget my keys.

    –ent   –ence   –ency

6. Good govern_____ is important in a political system.

    –ant   –ance   –ancy

7. I need your guid_____ about what to do next.

    –ant   –ance   –ancy

8. Americans have a life expect_____ of over 70 years.

    –ant   –ance   –ancy

Name _____

Recognize Root Words with Spelling Changes

> Read the first sentence in each pair. Look at the underlined word and identify its root word. Write that root word in the blank in the second sentence of the pair.

1. My teddy bear is very huggable.

   I love to _____ him.

2. To most people, one twin sister may be mistakable for the other twin sister.

   Their mother would never _____ one for the other.

3. A jeweler can valuate a diamond ring.

   That means the jeweler can determine the ring's _____ .

4. The candidates agreed the issue was debatable.

   Therefore, they would _____ it.

5. I find everything likable about him.

   I can't understand why you don't _____ him.

6. This chalk is erasable.

   My teacher asked me to _____ the whole chalkboard.

7. The tragic final scene is not forgettable.

   You will never _____ it.

8. That house with the broken windows and damaged roof is not livable.

   No one should _____ there.

Recognize Root Words with Spelling Changes

▶ **Read each sentence. Underline the word in the sentence whose root has a spelling change. Then write the root word on the blank below.**

1. The house is in a desirable neighborhood.

   root word: _____

2. The team quit the game because it was not winnable.

   root word: _____

3. It is not advisable to be outside in a thunderstorm.

   root word: _____

4. The late afternoon traffic was not avoidable.

   root word: _____

5. Two materials that can be melted together are fusible.

   root word: _____

6. This message is transmittable over the radio.

   root word: _____

7. We are fortunate to have good friends.

   root word: _____

8. This tube of toothpaste is squeezable.

   root word: _____

Name _____

Multisyllabic Words

▶ **Read each sentence and circle the word with the correct syllable division pattern to complete the sentence.**

▶ **Circle the word with the VCV syllable division pattern.**

1. I looked out my window and saw a _____.

  raccoon   robin

2. Jamie read a _____ about the legend of Atlantis.

  novel   chapter

▶ **Circle the word with the VCCV syllable division pattern.**

3. When he grows up, Rey wants to be a _____.

  lawyer   pilot

4. Kara _____ that she had to go first.

  complained   announced

▶ **Circle the word with the VCCCV syllable division pattern.**

5. Kendra's favorite subject in school is _____.

  science   English

6. Mike had a nightmare about _____.

  zombies   monsters

▶ **Circle the word with the VV syllable division pattern.**

7. In social studies, we learned about the _____.

  pioneers   Pilgrims

8. Alex learned about the accident on the _____.

  television   radio

Name _____

Multisyllabic Words

▶ Read each sentence, and then select the word from the box that makes sense in the sentence. Write the word in the blank. If you are unsure of a word's meaning, look it up in a dictionary.

disappointed	horrified	admitted	disqualified
radiation	calculation	contribution	recognizable

1. They were _____ to hear about the airplane crash.

2. She _____ that she made a mistake.

3. If you cheat, you will be _____ from the contest.

4. I know you are _____ that you didn't win.

5. The sun's _____ heats Earth.

6. You added the numbers wrong—check your _____ .

7. Zebras are _____ by their stripes.

8. Do you wish to make a _____ to charity?